Hello at Last

Embracing the Koan of Friendship and Meditation

Sara Jenkins

Windhorse Publications

Published by Windhorse Publications Ltd
11 Park Road
Birmingham
B13 8AB
UK
email: info@windhorsepublications.com
web: www.windhorsepublications.com

Cover Image: Women Drinking Tea © Image Source/Corbis
Cover design: Marlene Eltschig
Printed by The Cromwell Press Ltd, Trowbridge, England

British Library Cataloguing in Publication Data:
A catalogue record for this book is available from the British Library

ISBN: 978 1 899579 79 2

Contents

Hello at last.
You have only
just begun to
know each other.

Allan Gurganus

Preface
Getting To Know Us

'Deepen your relationships,' my Zen teacher said.

I had been complaining that my personality seemed always in my way, a sticky tangle of habitual reactions, a straitjacket of inauthenticity. 'How would deepening my relationships address a problem of personality?' I asked.

'I don't know,' my teacher replied, 'It just came into my mind, and it felt right somehow, so I said it.'

Deepen your relationships. I pondered that idea briefly, occasionally. But because my teacher discourages socializing among her students, it was easy to forget about it. Only as I began writing about spiritual friendship did it occur to me that that is precisely what I have been doing in the practices described in this book: deepening my relationships.

The Buddha actively promoted spiritual friendship, calling it, according to an ancient Pali source, 'the whole of the spiritual life.' But my teacher asks that her students not socialize with one another, and her monastery and retreats are conducted in strict silence. This apparent contradiction has been like a koan for me, that is, an intellectually insoluble riddle, based in paradox, that is used in Zen training to jolt the mind to a new level of understanding.

Friendship that flowers in silence, in the absence of social habit, is a cherished treasure: ineffable, mysterious, profound. Some of the early Buddhist monks are described in the Pali scriptures as living together in harmony, 'blending like milk and water,' and are said to have done so largely in silence, speaking only every fifth day.¹ In my experience, the awareness of deep relatedness that develops in silence is precious beyond description, but fragile, rarely surviving the shift to ordinary social interaction. The inward focus tends to dissolve the normal sense of boundary between the 'self' and all else. To the expansive, softened, unbound being, our usual degree and manner of self-assertion can be harsh. I refer to the multitude of ways in which we convey social identity: the fixed smile, the failure to truly listen, the flitting attention, the need to do, say, be something special. Those conditioned responses have the opposite of the intended effect; they sabotage our wish to be accepted by others, for it is precisely such be-haviour that sustains our sense of separation. Perhaps that is why my teacher encourages us not to socialize with each other.

I love silence and the fruits of silence, yet I have long sensed that an edge of my practice – where growth seems possible and even pressing – is in relating to other people. During silent retreat, a sweet, pure love unlike anything I have known wells up for the others who are there meditating with me; then, at the end of the retreat, our personalities take us over again – a sad spectacle. Without being fully aware of it, I adopted a koan drawn from my curiosity and my need, and based in the question implicit in my teacher's advice: how could I deepen my relationships – bring them into mindfulness – while not socializing with other students on the path?

As Buddhism has taken root in the individualistic societies of the west, practice has focused mainly on the personal quest for enlightenment via meditation. Now that many students are well grounded in sitting and walking meditation, there is a growing interest in *sangha*, or com-munity. Sangha is known as the Third Jewel of Buddhism. The word may be used narrowly to mean those who are ordained as monastics or members of a particular Buddhist group, but more generally it refers to the connectedness among all who follow the teachings of the Buddha, often called the 'Dharma' (meaning 'way' or 'law', in the sense of how things really are).

One way to foster sangha is through specific practices in spiritual friendship. Increasingly, spiritual friendship is an explicit component of Dharma groups, most notably the Friends of the Western Buddhist Order and Insight Meditation communities. In a thought-provoking essay, philosophical counsellor Greg Goode even makes a case for spiritual teaching to move away from the traditional 'guru model' towards learning that takes place primarily among friends.[2]

Like sangha, spiritual friendship is defined and manifested in a variety of ways, from the most general – closeness between people with a shared sense of some spiritual dimension – to the vipassana model in which highly advanced teachers are called spiritual friends. Except for the first and last chapters of this book, which deal with two very different expressions of spiritual community in my life, what I describe here are my experiences (my versions of those experiences, it should go without saying) with specific *practices* in spiritual friendship. These are mostly with individuals rather than a group, and with people who are my peers.

Spiritual friendships differ from ordinary friendships in that they are entered into consciously and conducted with a particular intention and within a particular context. Normally we choose friends who reinforce our identities, whereas friendship based on the shared aim of spiritual liberation works to soften the walls of self, to dispel the illusion of separateness. The familiar human terrain of disappointment, embarrassment, longing, trepidation, resentment, misunderstanding – in a word, suffering – is most fruitfully traversed with companions who are intimately familiar with those places in themselves. Sharing the light of mindfulness strengthens our ability to recognize our conditioned reactions as phantoms, to question them, to remember that in any moment we can turn our attention to what *is* real.

Spiritual friendship works in many ways. When my mindfulness fails, there's a good chance the other person's will be intact, a resource I may draw on. When I am tangled in ego reactions, I can go to a spiritual friend for help in loosening the knots. When both of us are trapped in suffering, at least we can remind each other of the larger perspective we share: freedom is possible, we can keep bringing our attention back to the present, and inevitably things will change. In the absence of suffering, we can enjoy the sweet practice of 'rejoicing in the merit' of others: taking pleasure in their abilities, in their sheer goodness; reinforcing that goodness by expressing our appreciation; and accepting appreciation when it is offered to us. At times, spiritual friendship can take on the exhilaration of a game as we observe each other and ourselves fencing with ego – a game hilarious in its absurdity, and liberating, as humour invariably is.

The spiritual friendship practices I know of are based mainly in what I think of as meditative dialogue or mindful communication. The practices described here, representing a variety of traditions, are elegantly simple, yet powerful enough to open our hearts to all of life. The elements of these practices are not exclusive to Buddhism; they often reflect trends in our culture, from the empowerment of women, with their natural propensity for 'tending and befriending', to the development in many areas, including psychology and the arts, of methods emphasizing self-reflection. A simple example is the guideline an actor friend of mine uses in a workshop on autobiographical storytelling: responses to each person's story are given in the form 'I felt/ noticed/learned/wondered....' The approach is to listen attentively to someone else, then respond by describing our own experience – a formula implying *simultaneous acceptance of ourselves and another*. Very simple and very powerful.

Mutual acceptance lies at the heart of the practice of spiritual friendship, and it is what I mean by 'getting to know us'. What we learn about ourselves through meditation and mindful communication is not exclusive to us; it is how all human beings operate. Participating with others in honest, compassionate dialogue, we see ourselves reflected in ways we are unlikely to notice on our own. To know myself is to know you; to know you is to know myself. This is not to imply that the Buddhist concept of no-self is easily attained, but that in practice with others, the rough sense of separation, of difference, by which we know ourselves as distinct, is gently polished away, allowing ever more frequent glimpses of our ultimate oneness. Offering ourselves as mirrors for each other becomes a breathtaking act of love.

1

The Silent Sangha

For many years, I believed that my Zen teacher, Cheri Huber, gave short shrift to sangha, or spiritual community. I never knew her to refer to anything like spiritual friendship, except obliquely, through this chilling quotation tacked to a bulletin board at her monastery:

> Those who, being really on the Way, fall upon hard times in the world will not, as a consequence, turn to that friend who offers refuge and comfort and encourages the old self to survive. Rather they will seek out someone who will faithfully and inexorably help them to risk themselves, so that they may endure the suffering and pass courageously through it, thus making of it a 'raft that leads to the far shore.' Only to the extent that we expose ourselves over and over again to annihilation can that which is indestructible arise within us.

The quotation is adapted from *The Way of Transformation* by Karlfried Graf von Durckheim.[3] I've read those lines many times. Usually I stop reading when I get to 'annihilation'; from there on, it only gets worse, exhorting us to 'let ourselves be assaulted, perturbed, moved, insulted, broken, and battered....' How much more pleasant to read, for example, in Sangharakshita's *A Guide to the Buddhist Path*, that in spiritual community we can be 'ourselves as we are at our best and our highest ... even at our worst if necessary, but be ourselves completely, wholly, perfectly.'[4]

My teacher's style is forceful, even scary at times, yet it is always haunting with promise. It is based in monastic practice, strictly and literally so, given that the root word *monad* means one, single, solitary. At the monastery the silence and solitude seem all-pervading. The monks (male and female) live in secluded hermitages and, except for what we call functional speaking, most often necessitated by work, communicate through written messages. They also observe 'custody of the eyes', not looking at one another. The retreats Cheri leads around the country also follow that monastic model, in that each student is left alone to practise looking inward, to be fully present to his or her inner experience, free from the need to project a personality for others and to respond to others' personalities.

I have the greatest respect for that approach; the grounding in silence and solitude is essential to my own practice. However, it is in the nature of ego always to find something wrong, and I began to think that the trade-off for that silent 'privileged environment,' as my teacher calls it, was a neglect of sangha. Before I figured out that arguing with Cheri is a waste of time, I expressed my opinions as to how things should be done, and I probably had my say at some point about sangha, lack of. When those opinions went (mercifully) unacknowledged, I proceeded to do as I pleased, with mixed results.

With my teacher several thousand miles away, I embarked on a self-defined project of seeking sangha, the results of which were stunningly consistent: utter and repeated failure. (On the other hand, as Cheri says, if we're paying attention, there's no way we can make a mistake, because every experience offers us information about who we are and who we are not.) I began from a misguided premise: that to go forth into the world and be helpful to others would form some sort of connection between people, and that would somehow take the place of a community of practitioners. I had not heard of 'engaged' (activist) Buddhism then, and sangha was a nebulous concept. I thought of my spiritual practice almost entirely in terms of sitting meditation, which I expected to lead me through a standard progression of insights, culminating in enlightenment, or, since our tradition avoids the E-word, happiness, or, simply, ease. I had no idea how my relationships with other people would fit into the programme, but I interpreted bouts of post-retreat fervour as the desire to do good in the world.

Over a period of several years, I offered to help with all sorts of projects: sending meditation books to prisoners interested in Buddhism, raising funds for a retreat centre, editing Buddhist teachings translated from Tibetan, acting as a courier for Dharma materials from South-East Asia – each offer ignored or declined. I persuaded people I worked with to make sandwiches for a soup kitchen, only to be informed that the kitchen was inundated with food donations so would we please not bring more. I offered to stay with a brain-damaged child so that her mother would be free to buy groceries, but proved unqualified because I wasn't strong enough to lift the girl onto the toilet. When I helped serve Thanksgiving dinner at a large shelter for homeless people, so many airline attendants showed up – they were stranded in the city over the holiday – and so efficient were their ministrations, that we more timid Samaritans were asked to stand out of their way. My telephone call to Mother Teresa's local contingent was met with a curt announcement that no volunteers were needed. An inner city counselling programme initiated by a born-again ex-drug addict needed assistance in writing proposals for funding; I volunteered, but the group never obtained tax-exempt status. A friend asked me to help her lead a meditation group for caretakers of people with terminal diseases, but the programme fell through because meditation was considered too 'alternative'. The Red Cross even declined to accept my blood.

'Have you considered that you might be barking up the wrong tree?' Cheri enquired gently, 'Maybe the high-profile service project isn't for you. Maybe you should put your effort into something more ordinary. Closer to home.' *Really* close to home, she probably meant, as in focusing on the one person I truly needed to get to know and care for, myself – in her words, 'turning the stream of compassion inward'.

In a flash I saw a perfect opportunity both to do good and to look inward: I could spend time with my parents, give them the gift of simple kindness. Of all the people in the world, my parents were the most likely to appreciate my attention – and the most likely to trigger my unmindful, self-centred, conditioned behaviour reactions. I entered into the project with Cheri's guidance and quickly experienced for myself a vital insight in Buddhist practice: when I perceived my parents as difficult, if I looked carefully, I could find the source of tension or resentment or frustration within myself. Once I saw how my mental state was projected outward to colour the atmosphere around me, it was within my power to stop it. I was not always willing to do so, but I could no longer deceive myself about where the responsibility rested.

That was my first experience of how Dharma practice could illuminate my life in the world beyond myself.

With my initial misconception laid to rest, I became interested in extending my practice to my interactions with others. How, I wondered, could I carry into ordinary activity the mindfulness I experienced in sitting meditation, and to some degree off the cushion, though only when I was alone? As soon as I was with others, personality pushed mindfulness aside.

In spite of my interest in that question, when Cheri introduced exercises in communication skills, I was sceptical and dismissive. The main communication exercise practised at the monastery and on our retreats was 'reflective listening'. One person speaks, and the other listens then summarizes what was said. Our instructions were to use the same language, or at least the same keywords, that the speaker used. 'Say the same thing back?' I protested, 'That's so simple-minded, it's insulting!' Plus it smacked of self-improvement workshops, I thought; it wasn't really Zen. I wanted to use *my* words. Years passed before I recognized old friend Ego in that determination to be in control – so that I could project the image I wanted others to see. Beneath my reluctance to repeat someone else's words was the fear of appearing foolish, and beneath that, the fear of being dull, of 'having nothing to

9

say for myself'. A primal fear: where would *I* be without my self-expression?

Meanwhile, I stumbled onto specific exercises for cultivating spiritual friendship (related in the chapters that follow), and through those experiences, I came to understand the usefulness of the training my teacher had offered early on. Much of the value in reflective listening lies like an open secret in – yes – the very repetition of the other person's words. While the person who is reflecting back may feel that the repetition is artificial and mechanical, people hearing their own words reflected back to them are so gratified that they scarcely notice. Summarizing what has been said in different words doesn't work as well; using the same vocabulary is what assures people that they have truly been heard. Of course, reflecting what others say with the sincere intention to understand and support them in communicating their concerns is likely to be more effective than repeating the words with a sceptical or self-conscious attitude. Still, with my own scepticism and self-consciousness operating at full force, I have seen again and again that the repetition itself conveys what we all want: acceptance.

After practising reflective listening for a while, I discovered its even greater value for the one who does the reflecting. The presence of the other person is a powerful incentive to mindfulness; with someone counting on me for the gift of full attention, I do not drift off into daydreaming as I might in sitting meditation.

Here is an interesting paradox. It seems as if repeating the other person's language would preclude spontaneity, which we tend to equate with genuineness. But, in fact, the use of *their* words instead of our own frees us from the constraints of our conditioned patterns, enabling a flow of heart-wisdom between two people that cannot happen when they speak from ego. In reflecting back what others say, we touch the essence of Buddhist practice: when we serve simply as a mirror, there is no space for the illusory self that keeps us separate.

Although I have never heard Cheri mention spiritual friendship, I remember the first time, one of the few times, that I heard her talk about sangha. She was about to lead a ten-day retreat that would culminate in retreatants accepting the Buddhist precepts as spiritual guidelines. The day before the retreat was to begin, she was diagnosed with Graves' disease, a form of hyperthyroidism. Everyone who had registered for the retreat was notified that two senior students would lead the daily schedule of meditation and discussion of the precepts, but whether or not Cheri would be there to lead the final ceremony, the culmination of the retreat, was uncertain. All the retreatants came anyway.

We face the wall for sitting meditation, and Dharma discussions always begin with Cheri silently – and, to us, invisibly – entering and taking her seat at the front. Then, at some point, she says softly, 'Would you please turn and face this way?' On the fourth day of that precepts retreat, the discussion began with one person saying that she kept hearing in her mind those familiar words, but in Cheri's absence, *please turn and face this way* meant to turn inward, to face ourselves, to find the teacher within.

The next evening we entered the meditation hall as usual, took our places, and sat in stillness. The windows and doors were open, and the warm autumn evening was filled with insect sounds. We sat for a long time. Some promise in the air held us, just sitting and breathing, in the peace and perfection of each moment.

Soft scrape of the screen door. Rustle of long heavy skirt moving to the front of the room. Perfect stillness. Insect music.

Then the whisper, 'Would you please turn and face this way?'

Cheri was thin and pale, her eyes unnaturally large and bulging. People later described their distress at seeing her so obviously unwell, but the stillness only deepened.

'This retreat is providing us all with a powerful experience of sangha,' Cheri said, her voice softer than ever but clear as a bell. 'Sangha is the community of followers on this path. All of us are teachers. We become our own teachers, and we are teachers for others. Not long ago, someone who had attended a retreat here drove across the country to our monastery, with the mistaken idea that ending his suffering required my presence. I wasn't there when he arrived, and he was upset. Fortunately, he stayed long enough to see that everybody at the monastery is a teacher, everybody becomes a teacher, including him. So, it is essential that we not confuse the person with the practice. Inevitably the person will go. It is the practice that remains.'

During the next few days, those of us who had already taken the precepts met with Cheri to work out procedures for the ceremony. Cheri's style of planning, to put it in the best light, allows space for people to operate from in-the-moment awareness. That is, I suspect that she deliberately leaves gaps and uncertainties in plans as openings through which we can rediscover that life cannot be controlled – because only when we relinquish the illusion of control are we free to participate fully.

Because Cheri was not well enough to lead the walking meditation that constitutes a large part of the precepts ritual, the plan was modified so that three of us would take turns. I was to lead the whole group of twenty-two people from the meditation hall at the beginning of the ceremony. I would rise from my cushion, walk to a low table near the door, light incense and recite some words, bow, leave the hall, and walk a few yards down the path. There I would stand in such a way that the others, once they had completed the same procedure and come outside, would know to form a line behind me. Each time another person came out of the hall, I would advance one step. When everyone was outside, I would lead the group to the site for the next stage of the ceremony.

Since we practise custody of the eyes, not looking at other people, I asked how I would know when everyone was in the line. When I no longer heard the door open and close, Cheri said, it would be time to go.

The morning of the ceremony was bright and cold and windy. I worried that being the first person in line for that first walk meant I'd be exposed to the cold longer than anyone ... but before that thought could settle into suffering, I let it go. Standing among the lichen-covered boulders and the towering poplars, gazing down a slope to an apple tree heavy with bronzed fruit and upward to swirls of golden leaves shimmering across the sky, I somehow knew that everything was and would be all right.

When about half the people had left the hall and I had advanced ten or twelve steps along the path, I could no longer hear the door open and close. After days of silence, with many entrances into and exits from the meditation hall, everyone had become adept at closing the door with no more than a soft scrape, lost in the roar of the wind.

Just like Cheri to leave me hanging – in charge but with no way of knowing what to do. Or, as she likes to say, with complete responsibility and no control.

I advanced a step. Maybe I could estimate exit times. And then add some time; the only problem would be if I left too soon. I resolved to wait as long as I could. In fact, I realized, it would hardly be possible to wait too long. Waiting in stillness is something Zen students are good at.

Another step. Standing. Breathing. Sound and touch of wind. Fragrance of apples. Awareness expanding to encompass air, leaves, trees, rocks, sunlight, sky. Others standing unseen behind me, still others coming to join the line. Our teacher remaining alone in the meditation hall.

After a while, I realized that the sensible thing would be to turn around and see if I could tell whether everyone was out. Custody of the eyes has to do with not interfering with other people and not allowing their presence to interfere with being present to yourself – not with blindly refusing information you need. And meditation itself is about looking, seeing what is so, not about rules and beliefs and assumptions, or pretending you know when you don't, or hoping against hope and reason.

I turned and looked. From the end of the line, someone leaned out and gave me a nod.

I never found out how long we stood there after everyone had come outside. It didn't matter. As the teacher says, there is no way you can make a mistake. If you don't know what to do, someone else is there to give you a nod.

Even in silence, sangha happens.

Here is how I envision my relationship with my Zen teacher. We are on a train, the train of Dharma, rolling through life, seeing what is, how things are. She is the engineer. I am riding on the platform at the back of the caboose. Our train speeds through peaceful plains, frightening storms, breathtaking scenery, and, yes, some stretches of terrain I consider boring. Now and then I entertain thoughts of disembarking at the next station. Then I remember: this is a train that never stops.

From the engine, the teacher leans out and calls back to us passengers, pointing out features in the landscape, drawing our attention to a river we are approaching, a waterfall, a mountain range.

'River!' I hear her call out.

'I don't see any river,' I grumble, fixedly looking out from the back of the train.

As we round a curve, my attention, which has been locked onto where we've already been, is drawn to the front of the train, and I see the teacher pointing off to the right. 'Look – waterfall!' she calls.

'Where?' I cry out, 'I don't see it. *Where is it?*'

'Look where I'm pointing,' she replies, 'Just *look.*'

Then the caboose bumps onto a bridge, and I look down into water. Oh, the river – here it is! By the time the teacher yells, 'Up ahead, mountains!' I've glimpsed the waterfall. And on we go.

Every time she points out something I don't see, I think she's deliberately tormenting me, or exaggerating, or just plain deluded. But eventually my experience catches up to her words, and I see for myself – ah, *that's* what she meant. Until that point, her travelogue is as maddening as a string of koans, the Zen riddles pointing towards what we most long for, and utterly resistant to reason.

Recently, several weeks at Cheri's monastery shed new light on my old koan, how to deepen my relationships without socializing in the sangha.

Each time I arrive at the monastery, I instantly feel embraced by the silence. After I've been there a while, I sense something even more precious because it is so rare: the intimacy between those whose silent practice brings them together physically, emotionally, and spiritually every day, without the filter and armour of a social persona.

On that last visit, I had come to the monastery to edit a book by the head monk. Our meetings to discuss his manuscript were conducted with a certain formality. We agreed to treat our discussions as mindfulness practice, and to that end, we met in the zendo and sat on our meditation cushions, facing each other. Our stated intention was to watch for the arising of ego – and if ever there is occasion for that, on both sides, it is between author and editor. Implicit in our agreement was that we would accept in compassion whatever arose, to the best of our ability.

He had created a structure for the book based on numerical harmony and a conceptual scheme that made a certain sense, but which from my point of view seemed inhibiting. That is, I saw his structure as precluding what I wanted: more dramatic development. I knew I was right; after all, I am the editor. On the other hand, he didn't get to be head monk by caving in, and, gently but firmly, he held his ground.

Each of us laid out our ideas about the book, examining them for unquestioned assumptions, holding them up to the light of our attention, maintaining awareness of our internal experience. We gradually came to see how our opinions, no matter how strongly felt and persuasively presented, were direct expressions of our conditioned personalities. He likes balance, for example, and I like drama – in writing and in life. His style is poetic, mine more direct. He favours an all-inclusiveness that I think of as rampant pack rat; when it's someone else's writing, I blithely favour minimalism. Each of those preferences is fully defensible but ultimately – literally – *self*-serving. Once that ego element was clear to us, we could let go of our preferences to make space for what served the book. What emerged most often as the best solution was something neither of us had considered. The more we let go, the more it seemed that the book itself was leading us to its natural form; we just relaxed, sat back, and watched it happen, awestruck. In my line of work, that is the ultimate joy.

On some occasions each of us took refuge in reflective listening, repeating back what the other had said, rather than expressing our own opinions. That way the other could hear the words afresh, rather than needing to defend them. (It really does work like magic.) We were focused, we were kind, and we were open, to a degree far beyond my expectation. We may have come to our cushions with various anxieties, but by the end of each session we were sitting there in full respect and trust and love.

I remember thinking, *This is how I want to be with people*, a thought that has often arisen in my experiences with spiritual friendship.

I did not intentionally set out to deepen my relationships, but the deepening process seems to be proceeding on its own. Communication is at the heart of it, inner stillness the foundation. My work with the head monk is one example of many in which I have consciously undertaken to develop my ability to be present with others. It's much easier, of course, with people who share that aim, but the capacity, at least, seems to be growing even in ordinary interactions.

As our Dharma train continues on its journey, from my post at the back of the caboose, ever more expansive vistas unfold. I remember more often to look towards where we're heading, and to the sides and below and above, not just where we've been. It slowly becomes clear to me that all along this train has carried the precious jewel of sangha.

Here, now: other people

Next door a lawnmower starts up, and I react with irritation. I want this day to be silent.

Kristen, a young Dharma student, has come to my house to work with me, as a meditative practice for us both. Our agreement is to work in silence, maintaining mindfulness as best we can and being aware of whatever distracts us. Before we begin working, we spend half an hour in sitting meditation.

Our cushions face open windows, under which the neighbour's lawnmower bellows back and forth. At the root of my annoyance is embarrassment; I want Kristen to experience my house and our work together as quiet, serene. Meaning – of course – I want her to view me that way.

If Kristen weren't here, I might use the noise as an excuse to give up for now and meditate later. But she's sitting quietly, a living demonstration of what is possible also for me.

I relax. The noise is just sound, after all, not a personal attack. Gradually, as I bring my attention to just sitting and breathing, the sound fills my awareness, becomes my world. After a while I hear it as the music of the spheres, and when it stops, I momentarily feel a loss.

After a brief intermission, the lawnmower solo is followed by a duet, weed eater and leaf blower.

Silence is relative. There are other people in the world.

One of them sits beside me, steadfast in this noisy magnificent silence. In this moment, she offers me the grounding of sangha.

2

The Third Jewel

My first encounter with practices in spiritual friendship was completely unexpected. But this is a path of endless surprises, in which expectations are regularly demolished. I never expected, for example, to take Buddhist precepts. One of the first things that attracted me to the path of Dharma was that it was not a religion, and whatever religious accretions had attached to it over 2,500 years I thought I could safely ignore. Thus, when my teacher asked early on if I were interested in taking the precepts, I had said no.

One of the ten precepts in our tradition is not to speak ill of any religion, and speaking ill was a freedom-of-speech right I wished to retain. Whatever did not meet with my approval deserved my criticism, I thought, and religions in general fell into that category. It also seemed to me that while the Buddhist path might be superior, only Zen was the true way. Then, too, within the full spectrum of Zen, my teacher's brand was the only one I found acceptable. Although, come to think of it, even she could wander off into some strange ideas ... and then I saw what I was doing: it all came down to *my* ideas, to me. When I told my teacher about that insight, she said dryly, 'The Religion of One has the biggest membership in the world. It's what almost everybody follows. Now, if you are sufficiently humbled by that awareness you just had, there shouldn't be a problem with taking a precept not to speak ill of other religions.'

But I had another, better reason not to take the precepts: I did not wish to assume yet another self-definition. How unassailably Zen! Never, I thought, would I identify myself as Buddhist, which would imply exclusion. My teacher saw it differently: the precepts ceremony was merely a formal acknowledgement and potential deepening of the practice I already followed, which was, in fact, Buddhist. I took the precepts, but my attitude about being labelled 'Buddhist' was still unsettled.

Soon after that, I spent several months with my brother, who was living in a Buddhist country, Sri Lanka. I remember emerging from the airport into the dark embrace of night-time heat and humidity, the smoky-flowery fragrances of the tropical air, the crowds of sarong-clad men drifting softly through the dark, the silent slow-motion grace of bicycles, pedestrians, and animals on the unlit road. I felt at once oddly at home and on the brink of an adventure. If I had been asked what I thought that adventure might be, my mind would probably have turned to some exotic aspect of the foreign culture, or some mystical experience related to my accepting the precepts. I could not have guessed that the adventure would unfold within the most ordinary human experience, opening a new direction in my path that has enriched my life ever since.

I arrived at my brother's house at 5 a.m. Along with the key, he had left a note saying that he was away and that the cook, Padmini, would arrive at 8 o'clock.

I unpacked and changed from my high-necked, long-sleeved layers of protection against airline chill into a light cotton nightgown. I knew exactly where I wanted to go: the second floor veranda where my brother had written that he watched the sun rise every morning. Beneath his folding chair, I found mosquito repellent and an object I realized, belatedly, was a doorstop. The door closed behind me with an implacable thunk; its vertical iron bolt had dropped into a slot in the floor. I was locked out.

Not a problem, I told myself. I am locked into paradise. Dawn is coming, and I will be present to the miracle of a new day.

Above coconut palms and frangipani trees and red-tiled roofs, the sky turned pearl and then peach. The air filled with birdsong, the early morning chatter of unfamiliar creatures, the fragrance of mock-orange blossoms and spicy breakfasts being cooked in nearby houses. Slowly, then quickly, light coloured the world, and day burst grandly onto my senses. Being locked out felt like a blessing, an enforced mini-retreat to slow me down to the gentle pace of that part of the world.

But impermanence lurks in paradise like the snake in the Garden of Eden. Even that early, the sun was getting hot. I moved the chair into a small patch of shade under a trellis of bougainvillea. The delicate colours of dawn began to blanch in the intense sunlight. The humidity became suffocating, and my nightgown stuck to my skin where sweat pooled. I needed to go to the bathroom. Not desperately, not yet, anyway. Sit very still, I told myself. But the equanimity I had embraced (or imagined) only a short time earlier had deserted me.

I considered my options. Trying to climb down a drainpipe in my nightgown seemed inadvisable, a feat performed by miscreants in movies, not by women of a certain age, not in places where they would be considered members of the memsahib class. As for calling out, what would I say? And if someone responded, even in English, what would I do then? Best to wait until Padmini arrived. Whenever waiting is required, I am grateful to know about meditation. Meditation means you're never at a loss for something to do, plus a certain self-assurance is born of surviving all those retreats. I settled onto the chair and turned my attention to my breath.

A clock chimed, without revealing the hour. Some immeasurable time later, the clock chimed again. More time passed.

At last I heard the gate creak and light footsteps come up the drive. I rose and looked down on a small brown woman approaching the back door. 'Padmini,' I called, 'I am here.'

She looked up, surprised. Then her face opened in a smile. 'Madam come,' she said.

Padmini's English could be ambiguous where declarative, imperative, and interrogative were concerned, but there was no mistaking the welcome in her face. And a minute later when she had come upstairs and unlocked the door, there was no mistaking her pride as she announced what she must have thought was the most important fact about herself.

'I am Buddhist,' she stated, beaming.

I had no way of knowing what she intended by those words. In a country with a long-running civil war between factions identified by religion, perhaps she felt the need to establish her allegiance at the outset, though that would not explain her glorious smile. Maybe my brother had mentioned my taking Buddhist precepts, except that I didn't think I had told him about it.

In any case, as I stood there in the bright, high-ceilinged hallway of a strange house in a strange country halfway around the world, filled with relief and gratitude at having been released from my prison in paradise, the simple human urge to connect made me want to blurt out, 'I am Buddhist, too!' But Padmini's Buddhism was bound up in ethnic and nationalist associations, and my claiming spiritual kinship would only perplex her. So I just smiled and nodded, and we walked in barefoot silence down the stairs to the first floor, where I turned into my room – a suite of rooms, actually, my memsahib quarters – and she headed back to the dim, cramped kitchen.

Years earlier, on my way to the Ajanta caves in central India, I had met an Indian man who told me he was Buddhist. That puzzled me: I knew little about Buddhism but understood that it had long since disappeared from India. My friend told me to read *The Buddha and His Dhamma* by Bhimrao Ambedkar, and insisted on arranging lodging for me in the Ladies Hostel at Milind College, not far from Ajanta. The

21

staff and students there were wonderfully friendly – warm, generous, open, kind. Later, reading about Ambedkar, I realized that he had founded the small college, and the people I had met there, as well as my friend, were former 'Untouchables' who, under Ambedkar's influence, had converted to Buddhism. After my visit, I had received a letter from the girls in the hostel:

> Dear Madam,
> We are very enjoy to meet you. Because you are first foreigner in our hostel. It is very enjoyable thing that you have behaved like sister. We all hope that you will not forget us. We also promise that we will not forget you never. Thanking you madam.
> Yours sisters.
> Milind Ladies Hostel.
> Aurangabad.

I liked being seen as sisterly, but being called 'Madam' made my heart sink. For the girls it was merely a polite form of address, but for me it was burdened with colonialism, the long exploitation of their sort of people by my sort of people. Given the difficulty of remaining mindful in social interactions in general, and the resulting shortfall of authenticity in relationships even with people very much like myself, true friendship between me and those girls, or any of the millions of people like them around the world, seemed highly unlikely.

That long-ago stay at the Ladies Hostel might have remained no more than a poignant travel memory, except for two subsequent events in the same general category of Buddhists turning up in unexpected places. First, and most surprising, I myself had taken up Buddhist practice. Second, my partner, Peter, discovered that the English vicarage where he had grown up had become a retreat centre for a Buddhist group, the Friends of the Western Buddhist Order (FWBO), founded by the English Buddhist, Sangharakshita. A magazine Peter brought back from England mentioned Milind College and gave names and addresses for centres in India where FWBO groups conducted social-work projects and taught Buddhism. Before leaving for

Sri Lanka, I had written to the main group, asking if I might visit their centre at Dapodi, outside Pune, to interview members for a magazine article.

I was resigned to not hearing before I left; when I did imagine receiving a reply, I half expected it to be a blue aerogramme penned in a juvenile scrawl, like the note from the Ladies Hostel. But a letter inviting me to come arrived promptly, typed on handsome letterhead and written in polished English.

I went to Dapodi with the idea that Indian Buddhism must share with its American counterpart that vitality that often characterizes a religious tradition taking root – or, in the case of India, being revived – in a place where it is not enmeshed in the culture. On the other hand, because American and Indian social situations are so different, I assumed that the teachings would be presented differently. As it turned out, what I found was on another level entirely: my first glimpse of how friendship can be actively practised as a fundamental part of spiritual life.

The white buildings of the Buddhist centre in Dapodi, garlanded with flowering trees and shrubs, sparkled in the dusty landscape. On the edge of a crowded urban neighbourhood, the complex struck me as an oasis in reverse: amid teeming surroundings, the relief of empty spaces. And, as I was to discover, amid the myriad divisions of caste, it offered true community. The very spaciousness of the buildings and grounds seemed to express the ease and trust in which friendship blooms, in which people can come together in the awareness that *everyone*, without exception, possesses the potential for enlightenment.

Although I was there only briefly, the time I spent in Dapodi has stayed with me to a remarkable degree. That is partly because I was relatively new to Dharma practice and because I was hearing Buddhist teachings in a new context. Also, transcribing and editing the interviews I recorded there burned the words into my mind. Over the years, as my experience caught up with what people there told me, phrases and sentences I had heard then would come to mind, and often I grasped what I had only glimpsed before. *A Dharma friend whom we trust entirely, from whom nothing is hidden.... When we are confused, a really deep friendship can be the one hook that keeps us connected.... Slowly, slowly, we get to know each other.... We need each other.*

The first person I spoke with at the Dapodi centre was Chandrashil, an Indian man whom I remember as being in his late middle age, with a broad, placid face. We sat together in a small room, and he described his work, training men for ordination. Right away he mentioned spiritual friendship. I had never heard of spiritual friendship and asked what it was.

Chandrashil looked perplexed. 'Surely you must know the Third Jewel,' he said softly, with the characteristic Indian wag of his head. 'Buddha, Dharma, and Sangha! Sangha is the community of followers, and in our community we are practising spiritual friendship.' By way of explanation, he recounted the story of Ānanda, the Buddha's beloved disciple, who noted that 'half the spiritual life is spiritual friendship, spiritual association, spiritual intimacy' – to which the Buddha is said to have replied, 'Say not so, Ānanda, it is the whole of the spiritual life.' [5]

Then Chandrashil began talking about communication. The FWBO approach, I gathered, not only emphasized sangha but promoted its explicit development, largely through the cultivation of spiritual friendships.

It was hard for me to fit that into my concept of Buddhist practice. My Zen practice centred on meditation and working with my teacher, whom I saw only a few times a year, and we students saw each other almost exclusively at silent retreats. It was my turn to be perplexed. What did communication have to do with Buddhism? I asked Chandrashil.

'We cannot separate communication and Buddhism,' he said, 'As you are talking to me and I am talking to you, we can see that you are a human being and I am a human being. There is no hierarchy, no class structure, nothing is there [to separate us]. Everybody has the same right to communicate on the human level. And we need to express what is happening, whether it is a good feeling, bad feeling, whatever it may be. If you talk about it, energy becomes released, you become relaxed, and communication happens very easily. Between friends, there is nothing hidden, you are not afraid of talking about anything, so you just become more and more open. You become a natural person.'

Chandrashil described specific formalized practices, for example, communication exercises that are given to new members of the community. In one exercise, two people face each other and look into each other's eyes for five minutes. This exercise is not uncommon in the west, and those who have participated in it can attest to its power. In another exercise, one person in a pair repeatedly says a meaningless sentence, such as, 'Water is wet,' and the other replies, 'Yes,' or 'OK.' In another, each person in turn speaks a sentence, and each gives full attention to listening to the other.

I found it hard to imagine the benefit of speaking meaningless phrases, and the exercises in general – the whole idea of such exercises, in fact – struck me as odd. But Chandrashil's manner in presenting them was so straightforward, so quietly engaging, such a perfect blend of warmth and clarity, that my scepticism was suspended. He seemed almost transparent, in that I could detect nothing operating in him but innate intelligence and kindness. He was offering me a description of their practice, not a prescription, yet he himself was a compelling testament to the effectiveness of that practice. The qualities I saw in him, that calm and that wisdom, were what I sought for myself – to be a 'natural person'.

Holding my gaze, in a completely easy and open way, he talked about how spiritual friendship might evolve from the communication exercises. 'As communication grows between us, then naturally I ask about you, and you ask about me,' he said, 'So, slowly, slowly, we get to know each other. What we see as differences between us exist only because you think you are separate, and I think I am separate. But with communication we can know each other. Slowly, slowly I see how you are like me, you see how I am like you, and there is no difference between us.'

Such simple words, such profound implications.

The director of the centre was an English disciple of Sangharakshita, Lokamitra. Lokamitra began our interview by describing sangha as a supportive environment in which we can be totally at ease in working towards what is highest in us. Unless we can be thoroughly open, he said, it is difficult to come to terms with the untransformed aspects of ourselves.

'We need to be able to look at [such aspects] with the concerned objectivity of a dear Dharma friend, whom we can trust entirely, who is not going to exploit our weaknesses or manipulate us through them, as in the usual worldly relationships,' he said, 'We need to be able to confess our shortcomings and weaknesses, not in an automatic and formalized way, but as a response from what is highest in ourselves to the difficulties we encounter in our practice.'

In any relationships within the sangha, Lokamitra noted, the point is not to give advice or solve problems, but to develop deep trust and genuine friendship. In the case of a more senior student befriending a younger student, each gives in different ways. The senior person may give more in clarity, inspiration, and commitment, and the younger in the energy of 'beginner's mind', raising questions about matters that senior students may take for granted, pushing them to rethink, reconsider, see with a fresh perspective. Friendships between people at the same stage of development are equally encouraged. During periods of confusion and doubt, Lokamitra observed, sangha can be crucial:

> Until a certain point on the spiritual path, Māra [the force of evil or ignorance; the devil] is stronger in us than Buddha [the force of awakening]. This means that we are pulled between worldly and Dharmic directions, and it's easy to become confused. But the confusion can be offset by spiritual friendship in the

sangha. For example, if I am thinking of making some change in my life – leaving my family for a year to go on a pilgrimage or start a new centre somewhere else – I wouldn't just go ahead and do it, I would discuss it with my spiritual friends. Even someone whose spiritual practice is less developed than ours can help us by saying, 'Oh, but did you consider this aspect of it? And what about that?' You can't listen to someone unless there's trust, and you can't trust someone unless there's a friendship there, a basic common feeling. I might not always like what I hear, but in the end I will take it seriously from a friend.

The more we practise, the more interest Māra seems to take in us. In a way, Māra doesn't have any work to do when we're not trying at all. It's only when we start making an effort that Māra comes into action, and then doubt may arise, with all its ugly relatives: resentment, jealousy, laziness, and so on. I'm fairly convinced that doubt comes to just about anyone on a spiritual path. We may doubt the teacher, or even the Buddha and the Dharma; we may doubt the meditation practice we are doing; we may doubt ourselves. If we are not careful, the doubt can go so deep that we begin to cut ourselves off from others who are practising the Dharma, to see them as an ordinary organization rather than as our spiritual community. Doubt means we no longer see the spiritual side, because we've lost that in ourselves. When we are confused, we're the last people to see it. And a really deep friendship is often the one hook that can keep us in contact with Buddha, Dharma, and Sangha.

It seems clear that the lack of focus on sangha in many western Buddhist groups reflects the absence in our society of the connections between people, the interrelatedness of community, that is taken for granted in traditional societies. Lokamitra put it bluntly: 'One needs friends in the world; one can get very lost without friendship. That is very much the case in the west, where many people are so lonely. Friendship should be the hallmark of sangha. If we cannot find it in the sangha, where will we find it?'

Of course we need friends, I thought, but I don't know about people being lonely. I didn't feel lonely, and I doubted that anyone I knew gave it a thought. It is a truism that the extreme individualism of western society produces fractured families, but whenever this is mentioned, I think about how I *like* individualism, how I would not want to live under the constraints of, say, a traditional Indian extended family. But Lokamitra's words stuck with me. Is there an isolation that we in the west don't see because it is a given? Is loneliness the water we swim in, the air we breathe?

When I talked further with Chandrashil, I saw that his community held an ideal of friendship, of relatedness, beyond anything I had ever considered. His words – so spare, so direct – seemed to pierce to the heart of human connection:

> In Buddhism, discrimination between yourself and others vanishes. You are taking some sort of food, I am taking some sort of food; you are having feelings, I am having feelings. All these feelings are the same between us two persons, so subject-object duality is finished. I don't bear a grudge to any person, because they are having the same experience which I am having. You may be from a different class, from a different country, maybe from England, maybe from India, from any place, but you are a human being, you have got the capacity to grow.
>
> If you are trying to do that, slowly, slowly, your human heart will open up. We are all human beings, and we all are suffering – not because of some god but because of our own actions.
>
> Now, if we know the internal intention of our actions, we can change ourselves. So, when this is your ideal and my ideal – you want to know yourself, I want to know myself – the aim is the same, and we try to help each other.

Communication helps us see the good in others, and seeing their goodness helps develop those qualities in ourselves, Chandrashil explained. A term he used was 'rejoicing in the merit' of another, encouraging goodness by expressing appreciation for our friends' acts of kindness and wisdom. Simple verbal appreciation links both people in awareness of what is good, reinforcing and enlarging their capacity for goodness.

Chandrashil told me that candidates for ordination within the Western Buddhist Order select two members of the community as spiritual friends, called *kalyāṇa mitras*. The new student and the *kalyāṇa mitra* spend time together on a regular basis, getting to know each other. It's like an ordinary friendship, except that it is within the context of Dharma practice. That is, while the two people enjoy each other's company, they are bringing their attention back to the present, observing their inner reactions, examining their choices in the light of Buddhist teaching. The relationship is based in a shared ideal: each person supports the other in becoming more like the Buddha in action, speech, and mind.

Another WBO member, Padmasuri, told me about how the *kalyāṇa mitra* idea was embodied in her friendship with an Indian woman, an 'ex-Untouchable' who had emerged as a leader among the Buddhist women in India. (Padmasuri's work with the programme in India is recounted in her book *But Little Dust*.) Initially, the two women had communicated mainly through a translator; Padmasuri later learned Marathi. 'But we were dealing with more than words; we were able just to tune in with each other. Vimalasuri is as close a friend to me as many of my English friends, and I think I am the same for her.'

Padmasuri described spiritual friendship as getting to know another person at the deep level where there is a meeting of hearts. That requires time, attention, and conscious effort, she said, and the result is truly open communication in which 'you feel free, you feel you can speak about anything, you can be yourself'.

But spiritual friendship is not just being nice to each other, Padmasuri pointed out; it can also mean giving critical feedback. 'The aim is to encourage people's spiritual development. There's no point challenging someone unless you've got a positive vision of what that person really needs, and the awareness of the person's potential, which is enlightenment. That takes not only getting to know them but also confidence in yourself to be able to do it, as far as you're aware, from the purest motives in yourself. If I see something that is hindering a person and don't say it, I'm letting myself down, never mind the other person. The Buddha would have said it.'

Padmasuri recalled the passage in the *Cūḷagosiṅga Sutta* of the Pali canon telling of three young monks going off together, living and meditating in harmony, 'blending like milk and water'. 'The ideal is there in the early scriptures,' she said, 'this beautiful idea of people helping each other and caring for each other and wanting the best for each other and breaking down the barriers between each other. I think Sangharakshita brought that into our practice partly because he particularly felt the lack of it: he was so much a single practising Buddhist with various teachers and never really had a sangha. Some very exceptional people like Milarepa haven't had sanghas, but we're not Milarepas, most of us, and we need each other.'

After I had interviewed Lokamitra and Chandrashil, Lokamitra's assistant, Malati, suggested that we visit an educational centre their group was building outside a nearby village. Several of us set off together on the short train ride. In the village we bought soggy cheese sandwiches and tangerines, then we walked across a field to the construction site.

A young man in our group, Yogesh, suggested that we sit in the shade of a haystack to eat our lunch. When we had settled there, he pointed out a range of hills in the distance. We were facing the Bhaja caves, he told us, where Buddhist monks had lived in the second century BCE. The meditation hall at the new centre would be aligned to face the caves. Noticing how Yogesh and Malati and the others beamed proudly at mention of the caves, I wondered what it must be like for these new Buddhists to contemplate such ancient roots, to be part of a sudden flowering of a religious tradition that had been so long absent from their land.

They in turn wanted to know what Dharma practice was like in America. We compared notes on sitting practice, retreats, and teachers, then moved on to our personal struggles and insights: the usual reactions when life doesn't go as we wish, the contortions and distortions of ego in protecting self-image, how acceptance from others can help us let go.

Yogesh described their work in the world as the practice of compassion. 'The difference between our social work and all other such projects is that we do it for ourselves,' he said, 'not for the people we help. I was always interested in social work because I grew up in the slums, and I saw how people suffer. But what I felt then was pity, not compassion. When you try to help people out of pity, you want them to change, or at least to appreciate your effort. When you do the same act in a spirit of compassion, you are doing it for your own practice and are not attached to the response of the people you help.' He said that the pity that originally motivated him was also pity for himself, and he had found that acting from compassion for others is a good way of dealing with self-pity, of caring for the part of himself that needed care.

Each person I spoke with looked into my eyes and spoke gently and clearly, inviting me to be present with them in the same way. Each of them struck me as being what my teacher calls a 'social relief' – someone who is easy to be with, accommodating without being ingratiating, open without needing ego-tending. Of course, with time, I would have encountered their weaknesses, their blind spots, as mine would have become obvious to them. But what struck me most forcefully was that among people whose history and culture and daily life were so remote from my own, when we spoke about Dharma, we saw our experience to be the same. To receive spiritual wealth from people who have so little materially is, to say the least, thought-provoking. It was a long trip to discover, yet again, the deeply persistent habit of looking for differences, when oneness is always at hand.

Shortly after I had returned to my brother's house in Sri Lanka, the country celebrated one of its major holidays, Wesak, commemorating the birth, death, and enlightenment of the Buddha. The holiday traditions, featuring large, rather lurid displays of scenes from Buddhist stories, could hardly have been more foreign to my experience of Dharma. Still, my heart was touched by a simple experience of what I like to think of as sangha.

Even though I had not mentioned my Buddhist practice to Padmini, she was determined that I should participate in the festivities and took me to a special market to purchase paper lanterns to hang for the holiday. The ones we chose had cut-out patterns of the eight-spoked wheel of the Dharma in red, yellow, and white paper; we cradled them carefully in our laps as we rode home in a tiny three-wheeler taxi. That night, hanging the lanterns at the entrance to the house, struggling to fix candles in them and keep them lit against the breeze, then standing together in the street to admire the clear, warm glow, I felt a wordless love between me and this woman with whom I could speak only the simplest language, and, in both of us, love for something beyond our individual identities.

When I thought of Lokamitra and Chandrashil and Padmasuri and the work they had undertaken in the building of community – when I saw that work in social and political terms – it seemed thoroughly daunting, something I could never do. But when I thought of the simple practices in spiritual friendship I learned from them, it was as if one of those Wesak candles flickered in my heart. If I were going to be identified as a Buddhist, at least I felt that I was in excellent company.

Back at home, I discovered a modest wave of Buddhist culture breaking at my very feet. A couple I had known for ten years had started a Tibetan Buddhist centre in our neighbourhood, and there I attended a gathering of representatives from all the Buddhist groups in town, Asian and American. The purpose of the meeting was to plan a joint celebration for the following year's Wesak, the first to be held in our Midwestern American city.

As I sat on my black zafu among cushions in all colours and practition-ers from a variety of lineages, the joy in our shared presence was almost palpable. That moment marked a step towards my expanding my practice to include friendship, beginning to explore what it means to take refuge in the sangha, to find a place for Sangha alongside the jewels of Buddha and Dharma.

Here, now: connection

I sit on my porch, writing. From a few yards away, through a window that opens into my office, comes the click of computer keys.

After a while, a bell sounds through the window. I put down my notebook and pencil, take off my glasses, sit still, and bring my attention to the present, to the sensations of my weight in the chair, the air on my skin, the ambient sounds.

Kristen, who is at my desk, introduced the mindfulness bell into our working meditation. She recently returned from a three-month retreat with Thich Nhat Hanh, where the bell is a signal to stop what you're doing for three breaths and say to yourself, 'The sound of this bell brings me back to my true self.'

At the end of our work period, we meet to reflect on whatever mindfulness, distractions, and insights we experienced. I tell Kristen I find the bell helpful. I had expected it at regular intervals, though, and it seemed random. How did she decide when to ring it? I ask.

She rang it, she explained, when she became aware that she had lost her mindfulness.

A frisson of unexpected connection: the bell links us not through a preconceived construct, and not in some abstract oneness, but through our inattention – where most of us spend most of the time – bringing us together in awareness, in the movement to here and now.

Kristen, her bell and her being, are drawing me – more than I can know at the time – towards community.

3

On the Way to No-Self

The drive from my urban neighbourhood took me along a winding road through shady residential suburbs. I would be eager for our meeting, thinking ahead of myself, and at the same time settling down towards the deep, clear calm I always found at Susan's house. She would meet me at the door with a smile radiating welcome. Perhaps I saw, reflected in her face, my own happiness at being there. But my sense was that the happiness arose spontaneously between us, just as our friendship flowered, the natural result of our coinciding in time and space and at a particular point in our spiritual journeys.

Susan would lead me into the living room where a bay window overlooked a spreading oak tree and a slope of lawn. Next to the window stood two blue wing-back chairs, turned to face each other at a comfortable angle. The whole arrangement created a feeling of safety within limitless space – the same paradoxical quality we find in meditation.

When I had sat down in one of the chairs, Susan would bring an ottoman for my feet, an act that always touched me. It was not that she was mothering me (that's not her style, nor is it mine to accept mothering), but that she noticed little things that might make others more comfortable, and acted, it seemed to me, out of the sheer joy of *caring*. Her act seemed non-personal – not impersonal, but not exclusively for or about me. As a result, I did not have to feel beholden, to think up something equivalent to do for her, to make a special effort to ensure that she recognized the full degree of my appreciation, to assert my 'me-ness' against her 'her-ness'. I imagine it like this: two human creatures, one seated who would be more comfortable with her feet raised, one who knows where the ottoman is and brings it, the two of them embraced equally, impartially, in that reality. Along with the ottoman. And the chairs, the room, the tree, the lawn, and everything around and between and within.

In the same kind but non-personal way, Susan would bring in tea and cake or cookies, and in the same way we would begin to talk. To someone listening in on our conversation, it might have seemed quite ordinary in tone and affect, the easy, intimate, trusting talk that happens readily between women. But the intense focus I experienced in talking with Susan brought to mind *dokusan*, the interview, often highly charged, between student and teacher in the Zen tradition. With a shared aim of bringing to light the habitual unconscious patterns that drive our lives, Susan and I would sit facing each other in the quiet room and speak what was in our hearts. Being listened to with true interest and acceptance produces a space in which truth is free to tumble out, and that is precisely what happened, time after time.

'Wait – I am overdramatizing this,' I remember saying in the midst of some story I was telling Susan. On other occasions, I would become aware of adopting a dejected tone when nothing was really wrong; often, simply feeling tired became an occasion to indulge in generalized suffering. Such insights arose more readily in Susan's steady presence, and I would admit them with no hesitation. She in turn would catch herself in her own habit patterns, interrupting herself to say, 'No – that's not the whole story. Part of my motivation is how I will appear in other people's eyes.'

It went without saying that our talks were opportunities for bringing mindfulness – the moment-to-moment awareness we aim for in meditation – to personal interaction. Another given was that each of us has to do her own practice, arrive at her own insights; neither of us can save the other. Between giving and receiving there was no distinction; in bringing our full presence to listening and to speaking, we both gave and received simultaneously.

We would spend two or three hours in those blue chairs. We would offer ourselves up in the presence of the other to avail ourselves of whatever wisdom might arise, from whatever source. When the time was over, we both knew it, and I would leave.

It is only because of what I had learned in many years of working with my Zen teacher that I was able to participate effectively in that informal *dokusan* of peers with Susan. Without a firm grounding in silence, the clear and simple speaking that characterized our talks would have been hard if not impossible. Susan shared that grounding; she had come from two years of Zen practice at Shasta Abbey Zen monastery, whose founder, Jiyu-Kennett, had inspired and influenced my teacher. Another factor was that Susan and I both, to different degrees, perhaps, had seen beyond the illusion of one special person being the exclusive repository of spiritual wisdom. Wisdom is always at hand – not in the personality of the teacher or the rank of the monk, but in the simple act of attending deeply and responding from the heart.

And yet it was easier for me to recognize the capacity for such listening and such response in Susan than in myself. Many of us readily exult in the virtues of our friends but are reluctant or unable to discern our own virtue. In most ways, I see myself as a knowledgeable person with certain accomplishments, but I swing to the opposite side of the duality when it comes to Dharma practice: it's all but impossible for me to admit to any degree of spiritual development. Each time I dismissed my own merit, Susan would point out that I was one half of the clear and compassionate communication occurring between us. I began to envision her as a benign agent of my fierce Zen teacher, who not only refuses to go along with my hiding behind assumed (or feigned) inadequacy but calls to my attention moments when I act from a clarity that I-as-ego could never recognize.

The acknowledgement of goodness in other people is consciously undertaken as a practice in spiritual friendship. Whether or not they see their own enlightened nature, our pointing it out reinforces that awareness in us, and the pointing is not to you or to me or to them, but to that potential for enlightenment we share as human beings. That practice – 'rejoicing in the merit' of a spiritual friend, as it is called in Theravadin (South Asian) Buddhism – emerged quite naturally between Susan and me. What a concept: not only recognizing another's moments of illumination or steadfastness through difficult stretches of the path, but rejoicing to see the promise of the Dharma actualized in one of us. In *Buddhism for Today*, Dharmachari Subhuti, a member of the Western Buddhist Order, describes it this way:

> Real friendship involves an awareness of the other's potential. We do not simply see what they are but what they could be. Not only do we have powerful feelings of well-wishing towards our friends, but we hope that they will grow. Our friendliness would lead us to do everything we could to help them realize their potentiality. Real friendship is not need-based but growth-based and becomes fully possible when both friends are committed to developing as individuals.[6]

Later, I realized that *dokusan* was a less appropriate term for those talks at Susan's house than *kalyāṇa mitratā*, or the practice of spiritual friendship. Subhuti addresses a particular aspect of this:

> The process of stretching beyond oneself is particularly experienced in communication with those who are, to some degree, more developed than oneself. When one comes in contact with such individuals, *and if one is open to them*, then one shares for a while something of their experience. In this way one's own perspectives are broadened, one discovers new areas of one's own being, and new qualities are awakened in one. It is as though, in coming in contact with the qualities which one's friend embodies, those qualities are stimulated in oneself. This is Kalyana

Mitrata, or 'spiritual friendship'. Through one's friendship one is put in contact with a higher level of consciousness, which is actualized in one's friend and latent within oneself.

The principle of Kalyana Mitrata cannot be translated into an ecclesiastical hierarchy. One must discover through one's own experience who has developed in ways that one has not done oneself. Yet once one has found such friends and if one is able to open oneself up to them they are of inestimable value. Far better than words, practices, or symbols they offer a living reflection, however pale, however imperfect, of the Ideal.[7]

Susan and I were living in the middle of the United States when we met, both of us Zen students whose teachers were on the West Coast. We were given each other's names by a mutual acquaintance who taught meditation. For our first meeting, at a café near where I lived, I arrived early, happy to have a chance to browse in my new copy of *Buddhist America*. We hadn't made a plan for recognizing each other, so I propped up the book to display the cover. Susan saw the book, got the message, and came straight to my table. She says she sensed right away that we were embarking on a deep friendship.

We discovered many points of connection in our lives. It was surprising that we had not met earlier; for years our paths had crossed without our knowing it. We had taught at the same university and lived in the same neighbourhood, and later we had both lived in Washington DC, on opposite sides of Dupont Circle. When we finally did meet, I was living near a house where Susan had lived as a child. I passed it often; it stood out in the neighbourhood as especially pretty and peaceful. When I saw children there playing on a screened porch, I always thought what a perfect growing-up place it was – and was amazed to learn that Susan actually had grown up there. We marvelled at such connections; they might or might not be meaningful, but they were like spice in the sweet affinity between us.

In other ways, one in particular, Susan and I were very different. In the midst of a conversation we've both forgotten, Susan asked me what 'feminist' meant and whether or not I was one. I later understood that she knew the literal meaning of the word but she suspected that her sense of its meaning might be superficial and was interested in enlarging it by discussing it with me. At that moment, however, I was shocked. Because Susan and I attempt to practise 'Right Speech' with each other, I did not say, 'How could you be so appallingly ignorant and hopelessly benighted!?' but it must have been obvious that a thought of that sort passed through my mind.

Now, if I had been as mindful in that moment as Susan was, I might have noticed a characteristic in myself that often blocks a larger understanding of any issue: I want to *already* know what things mean. I place a high value on what I know and value my friends for what they know. Knowing makes me feel strong and safe; not knowing can be extremely uncomfortable.

'Feminist simply means being for women and the feminine,' I replied then, less confident than I sounded, 'so of course I am feminist.' The truth was that I had given little thought to what feminism meant. As part of the counter-cultural movement of the late 1960s and 70s that led me and many of my peers to meditation practice, it was something I took for granted. But Susan's openness to expanding her understanding was an invitation for me to consider it more deeply.

It seems to me that feminism and Dharma practice have in common a shift from other-identification to self-identification; that is, from blindly following conditioned patterns to seeing for ourselves what is so; investigating thoughts, feelings, actions to find out who we are, on the way to finding out who and what we are not. For example, reading that Elizabeth Cady Stanton (in *Solitude of Self*) spoke of 'the importance of fitting every human soul for independent action' and of 'the complete development of every individual',[8] I was reminded of similar language in Subhuti's book.

Within the FWBO's emphasis on sangha, spiritual friendship is an essential tool in personal development. I haven't heard of 'personal development' as an explicit aim in other Dharma groups, but it is implicit in the monastic training offered by my teacher, and, I gather from what Susan has told me, at Shasta Abbey. Subhuti describes candidates for higher spiritual realization as mature human beings, whose emotional stability no longer depends on factors outside themselves, which is one way of expressing the transformation I've seen in people who train as Zen monks under my teacher. As she succinctly puts it, 'It's very good to be in the driver's seat in your own life.'

What, then, of 'no-self'? As I piece together bits of guidance from my teacher with my own experience, the picture that emerges is something like this: we are unlikely to get beyond the notion of self until we have fully embraced our selfhood.

I think the same principle applies in feminism. Once you have embraced your nature and your worthiness as a man or woman, it's a short step to 'in Dharma there is no male and female,' which I take to be my teacher's attitude (Susan's as well; she got there ahead of me). And it's a natural step to compassion for all of us whose lives have been constrained by gender-determined roles, a compassion that arises more often these days (in me, at least) in response to men's situation than to women's.

In any case, a short time after Susan's question about feminism and my answer, she said she'd thought about it and decided that she was not a feminist, in that an active feminist agenda was not part of her life. In fact, it wasn't part of mine either, but had I still been operating on the assumption that my friends must necessarily share my political opinions, I might have used Susan's declaration to erect a boundary between us. By then, though, it was too late. Our hearts were already bound together in Dharma sisterhood.

That experience points towards something I cannot describe directly, something beyond the usual dynamics that draw people into friendship. Even though weeks or maybe months passed before I connected my visits with Susan to *kalyāṇa mitratā* practice, all that time, I believe, we were following a shared inner impulse to hold our friendship within a spiritual context, to offer it the chance to grow into something deeper than either of us had known, to take us further into the joys of expanding awareness that had become so precious through meditation. For me, that impulse was like the unspoken thought, *This is what I want more of in my life.*

Early in my practice I heard two ideas that express in different ways the Buddha's third noble truth, that there is an end to suffering. One is that Buddhism is based on the understanding that life is manageable. The other is a favourite of Cheri's, that 'suffering is optional'. The practice of spiritual friendship has been a way for me to experience that truth in an arena, close relationships, in which our conditioning is, however overtly or subtly, to armour ourselves with ego, where my me-ness is defined in relation to your you-ness. Practising mindful interaction with Susan opened a different door to the stepping aside, getting the ego-self out of the way, letting go – whatever we call that shift in consciousness that does indeed end suffering. It is as if her presence holds that door open when, on my own, I might not even notice a door is there.

Between Susan and me there evolved a custom of laughing at the increasingly predictable ways in which our egos assert themselves. We have come to know each other's conditioned patterns so well that we can refer to them in shorthand. An incident we now recall as emblematic of such shared self-knowledge occurred late one evening when we'd worked hard all day on a writing project. In drafting a biographical note for Susan, we disagreed on what to include. I was in favour of a less-is-more approach, while Susan didn't want to rule out the possibility that more is more. To support my view, I invoked an example I'd seen in a book, which, because of the source, I considered irrefutable. Then, becoming aware of my tendency to grasp onto information, especially published information, as a way of being right, of establishing my authority, my self, I said, 'As you know, my dear Susan, I am a person who wants to Know.' And Susan, aware of her tendency to want public acknowledgement, responded, 'And I, dear Sara, am a person who wants to Be Known.'

We collapsed into helpless laughter, mixed with tears, at the pathetic, persistent strivings of ego. In the subtle but crucial shift from suffering over how we are, to laughing about it – from viewing human nature as tragic and struggling against it, to accepting it as an ongoing comedy – my spiritual friend and I experience the healing release that happens again and again in Dharma practice.

After a year or so, both of us moved away, and we now live several hundred miles apart. We talk by phone and we visit, and the closeness that arose so quickly between us is undiminished. As I practise being present with Susan – a human creature in whose eyes I see reflected my own pleasures and pains – my armour softens and falls away. I learn, again and again, that however different our strategies may be, we operate from the same fundamental motive, wanting to be accepted. Occasionally we glimpse how in the most personal revelations, mine or hers, we are face to face with the non-personal. And in that awareness, we are emptied, momentarily, of self.

Here, now: a good idea

At noon, I suggest to Kristen that we make tomato sandwiches for lunch. She proposes that we practise mindful eating and offers to lead us in the form she learned on retreat.

We eat in silence, giving our attention to the sensory experience of the food. Alone together, such a sweet experience – sharing this time and place, this meal, yet immersed in our own experience, free to give it our full attention.

Halfway through, Kristen speaks. I feel a tad jolted, reluctant to leave the silence. But I see that she is easing into conversation by allowing mindfulness to inform our interaction. She expresses appreciation – 'rejoicing in the merit' – of the food and the company, which returns me to my experience, so that my own speaking can emerge naturally from what is happening in the moment. Gradually, seamlessly, we move towards talking as we normally would, but more mindfully. I am impressed with the skill Kristen brings to this delicate task.

I know Kristen because she started a meditation group that I heard about through friends. After her three-month retreat, she had left her job to devote herself to Dharma practice and was living with her parents while she looked for a spiritual community to move to. As an intermediate step, she wanted a sangha, so she spread word about a weekly gathering for sitting and walking meditation.

I had mixed feelings about getting into a group. I had done my time with groups, I believed. Not having lived near my teacher or any of her students, I never had the typical sangha experience of a more or less stable set of people following a particular tradition. But I had dutifully taken my teacher's advice to find somebody to meditate with – another Buddhist group or a solitary Dharma student or, in the absence of Buddhists, a Friends' Meeting. The group I eventually found had formed around two men who were students of different Theravadin teachers. The others who came were also long-time meditators who were beyond needing explanation or inspiration or encouragement. Our weekly meetings consisted of two hours of sitting and walking meditation, and that was all: no talk, no leader, no projects, no newsletter, no expectations beyond keeping the silence and staying still. It was easy for me to come and go without speaking, easy to avoid socializing.

But I had moved to a new place, and now here was Kristen with a very different approach: the weekly meetings at her parents' house included readings, mindful speaking and listening, and shared meals. Sometimes there was even singing and free-form walking meditation in which people might actually hold hands. And on retreat, Kristen told me, they had hour-long 'deep relaxation' periods after lunch. It sounded like kindergarten! Where was the rigour of Zen?

What I wanted in a group was clear to me. I was willing to let go the almost military strictness of my teacher's style, but I didn't want to meet on Sunday, which is my day for silence and solitude, and I didn't want to socialize. Most of all, I did not want to mix meditation practice and potlucks.

My friend Barbara had gone to the first meditation and urged me to come with her to the second, when people who were interested would discuss time, place, format, and so on. I went because I thought it would seem narrow-minded not to, but I did not feel inclined to relax my requirements. Nor did I think it likely that the group would meet them – whereupon I would have an excuse not to join.

To my surprise, the others who showed up at Kristen's agreed to all my preferences, leaving me no ground from which to resist. Still, I made no commitment; I was full of scepticism.

Driving home from that meeting, an idea formed in my mind, a way to tap into Kristen's experience and enthusiasm for Dharma practice without joining the meditation group. Kristen was tutoring a violin student and teaching a class in basic Chinese, but she wasn't really earning a living. From what I gathered, she spent most of her time at home, meditating and reading Dharma books. I needed help with house and yard maintenance and office work, but it was hard to find people to do those jobs for the money I could pay, plus I find it disruptive to have people in my small cottage while I am working. Kristen, I figured, would be grateful for any paid employment while she looked for a spiritual community. And her retreat experience meant that she was accustomed to silence and to the concept of work as mindfulness practice.

I emailed her my proposal: that she come to my house for as much or as little time as she liked, at pay slightly above minimum wage, to work on any of the tasks on my long list. She accepted. Joyfully, it seemed to me.

Such a simple idea, yet such a good idea. Quite beyond the practical benefits to both of us, there is the wonderful opportunity to practise mindfulness with another person. As we finish eating and clear the table, our talk subsides, quite naturally, as we return to work and to silence. I am filled with gratitude.

It's one-on-one practice that interests me, I tell myself. On this level, I actually can maintain mindfulness, whereas with a group I slip so quickly into the opposite. A real sangha is probably not something I'm ready for.

4

Faith and Freedom

Before I had heard of spiritual friendship, I was friends with a woman I knew through Zen practice, which we began at about the same time. She later took the spiritual name Faith. Just thinking of that – how she used to be Mary and how she has grown into her new name – makes me smile.

Until recently, I did not think of Faith as beautiful. There's a gap in her front teeth (a look that had not yet been rendered attractive by a popular model), and lissome she is not – she's bigger-boned and broader-shouldered than women you see in advertisements. But I didn't care about her looks; what appealed to me were her wild sense of humour, her clear-eyed honesty about herself, and her commitment to Dharma practice.

One of the things I like best in my friendship with Faith is the ease with which we move from playfulness to intense inner scrutiny. Our time together has always been on the fly, and we tend not to waste it in the automatic behaviours common to most social interaction. We can play with abandon – laughing, teasing, posturing – then sit down together to explore the most painful and threatening aspects of our ego-enslavement.

I envision that process as analogous to the Buddha's finding a Middle Way between the extremes of indulgence and deprivation. The middle ground we seek is often between extremes of self-conceptualization: *I am this, but I want to be that. People see me as one thing, but I am really another. How can I become A when someone needs me to remain as B? I long to be X but fear I am Y*. Such polarities – one thing versus another – pull us apart, not only from others but also within ourselves. As we observe our minds more closely, however, everything we think we know about ourselves is called into question and, ultimately, those conflicts resolve somewhere in the middle. Then we are simply here, existing in neither past nor future but now, beings whose conditioned ideas lose their power to limit us, once we find our way to this present moment.

The resolution of that sort of inner conflict is accompanied by a delicious burst of freedom. Faith and I can be in a playful mood or in the midst of some sombre ego examination, and up pops that freedom, scaring us for an instant, as startling as a jack-in-the-box – abrupt awareness, from who knows where, that we are not who we think we are. Not who we think we should be. Not the roles we adopted long ago and inhabit unquestioningly.

I had come to know Faith – back when she was Mary – mainly in silence, at autumn and spring retreats with our Zen teacher, Cheri. Those were seriously silent retreats. When a retreat was over, many people left in silence, and those who wanted to talk did so quietly where they wouldn't disturb others. Mary and I did not seek each other out, but if we met in a hallway or on a path, we would embrace. My sense was that our closeness in those moments arose from our shared experience: the deep mysteriousness of the journey we had embarked on, the extent of human suffering we were uncovering, our witnessing of the other's effort to free herself. We never said we would not speak at the end of retreats, we just didn't. After we embraced, we would look into each other's eyes, bow, and part.

I say I had got to know her then, yet several years must have passed before we talked. The only times we had spoken in each other's presence was in group question-and-answer sessions with our teacher, which in our retreats take the place of Dharma talks.

'What would you like to look at tonight?' our teacher asks. That invitation, students quickly realize, is not to analyse their lives or be clever or deliver a lecture or indulge in misery or blame or defensiveness. It is to turn our attention inward and see ourselves with fresh eyes. Mary amazed me in those sessions because she was funny without being a show-off, and she would reveal her suffering without wallowing in it. She knew herself, and her openness with that self-knowledge allowed us to know her, too.

Mary was on the board of the retreat centre, in charge of communication. When I was asked to edit an issue of the centre's newsletter, with her as my contact person, we talked by phone for the first time. It was fun working together. She pitched in beyond the call of duty, handling the layout and even drawing a cartoon to fill in a blank spot – a really good cartoon, with lettering that was at once whimsical and stylish. I was impressed.

The differences between us were for me a source of fascination and self-congratulation. In Mary, I saw a woman twelve years younger than I am, strong, blonde, handsome, an Amazon type, and a lesbian. I am dark, strung together with thin bones and loose muscles a physical therapist calls wet noodles, and hopelessly interested in men. As for being handsome, when someone occasionally applies the term to me, I am sceptical. Actually, I am hurt: at best I hear it as faint praise – I want to be more than handsome – and at worst as a euphemism.

From my point of view, however, the most striking difference between Mary and me has always been her confidence in areas in which I feel insecure, for example, being in charge of anything. What there is to be in charge of on our Zen retreats is largely physical work: deep cleaning, which I can manage, and construction, maintenance, and other projects involving skill and machinery, which intimidate me. At one memorable low point on a retreat, I was designated supervisor of a crew consisting of me and another person, charged with driving a mammoth wreck of a truck around to fifty or so cabins, collecting garbage cans, washing them out, and returning them. I was terrified at the thought of driving, especially that truck, on the steep, twisting mountain road. Furthermore, I was stumped when it came to planning how to return the garbage cans to the right cabins. (It sounds simple, but with different size cans and different size racks for them, there are ways to make a mess of it, believe me.) My crew member kindly made the plan and drove, and I served with reasonable competence in the role of heaving garbage cans on and off the truck. Mary, no doubt, could have done it all single-handedly. Mary built whole buildings, remodelled old ones, transformed nondescript interiors into jewels of comfort and clever design, scrubby yards into landscaped loveliness.

On the other side of the coin, I was immersed in a world of books and scholarship and high culture to which Mary seemed oblivious when she wasn't poking fun at its pretensions. I noted that she rarely talked about what she was reading, the mainstay of my identity, and her spelling often sprang loose from convention. Those and other telltale signs of the non-egghead I forgave, in part because I saw her as an artist. Her skill and taste found expression in everything she created. We loved comparing aesthetic judgements: would this look better here or there? Does this colour enhance or dull that one? Is this juxtaposition a fresh artistic statement or is it hopelessly hackneyed? Our pleasure in that kind of exchange lay in the affinity it revealed, which balanced out our obvious differences.

More significant, through Dharma practice, we were coming to understand that while the building blocks of our ego-constructed self-images might vary, the process is the same. We human beings unconsciously fabricate versions of ourselves and of one another that are compared in some Buddhist teachings to houses. The House of Sara, incompetent in the material world but confident in the world of books, conjures up a House of Mary to suit its purposes, to reinforce its own identity by way of contrast and similarity. Knowing that we were engaged in the same process of fabrication, however, Mary and I were able to meet in the middle, in the free space between those houses.

The first time I became aware of my friendship with Mary shifting to a deeper level was after our Zen teacher showed up at a retreat wearing earrings. Tiny, tasteful, but still … I hated it. And not on the grounds that they didn't work with the austere black robes. No. Much worse than that. Much more personal. Totally personal, in fact. Assuming that the earrings meant that our teacher wanted to look more feminine, I felt outraged, as if some tacit covenant had been broken. *Spiritual teachers aren't supposed to care about how they look.* Shortly after that, Mary visited me on her way across the country to Cheri's monastery in California, and I mentioned the earrings. I expected her to agree with my assumptions and thus bolster my sense of rightness, of self. But Mary simply looked at me and asked what exactly had upset me. My eyes filled with tears. In her presence I felt so safe, I guess, that the truth rushed out: *I* wanted to look more feminine, but made no effort in that direction lest I look foolish instead. Plus, I thought I *shouldn't* care about how I looked. In that moment, I not only realized something about myself, I also discovered that with Mary I had nothing to hide.

A friend from whom you have nothing to hide is precious indeed.

Mary went to the monastery to supervise a building project, and stayed on to become a monk. Rather quickly she was elevated to the position of Work Director, which among the monks carries the greatest responsibility and authority and pressure. I thought of her as Supermonk. It was a role she seemed destined for – carrying with it, of course, the supreme challenge of not believing in that role.

I was working on a book about monastic practice, based on interviews with the monks about their spiritual training. I arrived at the monastery expecting that the interviews would be conducted informally, perhaps in my dormitory room, where I envisioned lolling around on my bunk (not both of us, of course; the monk would need to be in the folding chair), being regaled with accounts of spiritual adventure, the high drama of monastic life. (Where do I get these ideas?)

51

The 'privileged environment' of the monastery – the strict silence and custody of the eyes, the inward focus – does not allow for anything like that, my teacher reminded me. The interviews were to follow the form of *dokusan*, the formal meeting between Zen student and teacher, or guidance, as we call it. I would see each monk for an hour, one after another, during their work periods. The two of us would sit facing each other in a room off the meditation hall. I would ring a bell to begin and end, we would bow to each other after each bell, and we would treat the whole thing as meditation.

I didn't exactly panic, but only because that's not my style. I crumbled inside. Even during *sesshin* (intensive meditation retreat), walking periods provide breaks from sitting. How could my body endure sitting all day? How could I maintain such intense engagement with another person hour after hour? What if some of the monks had nothing to say? What if the tape recorder broke? When would I go to the bathroom? I was convinced that I was not up to the job; I saw myself collapsing – splattered, almost, on the floor – humiliated. But I had endured other similarly daunting situations with Cheri, and an important lesson I had learned was that, in the face of a seemingly impossible task and the attendant fears, there's only one thing to do: give up and go along, and somehow everything will work out.

My interview with Mary was a demonstration of what I most needed to know for myself at that moment: that sincerity is a strong current that can carry you through dangerous waters and deposit you safely where you want to go. Mary described the difficulties of being Work Director with a candour that took my breath away. She didn't flinch from expressing her frustration about the double-binds in which she regularly found herself, nor from revealing the other side of her confidence, a corrosive self-doubt. She acknowledged her tendency to buy into others' image of her as the expert, the hero. She admitted the temptation to see herself as Supermonk, to believe in her special abilities. She confessed to thoughts and feelings that, coming from someone else, in a different context, would have embarrassed me: fear that she would be exposed as a fraud, not infinitely capable after all, sometimes not even knowing what to do next, at a loss; sadness that such fear still held her in its grip; the bitterness of self-recrimination.

For our interview hour, we sat there on our black Zen cushions, face to face, knee to knee. I watched and listened and participated as fully as I had ever participated in anything. It seemed as if the whole of our Zen practice were being laid out before me. Becoming aware of playing a role, then dropping it. Noticing conditioned patterns of clinging to an idea of who or what we are, and letting them go. Recognizing what stands in the way of letting go, and seeing the suffering involved. Occasionally Mary would move outside her account of suffering and laugh at it all, at the absurd drama played out by the self in its desperate effort to Be Somebody. Laughter in that situation could have been self-deprecating or bitter or a way to mask pain, but I heard in her laugh the same quality I heard in her admission of struggle: sincere commitment to be present in the gamut of her experience, from the tragic to the comic. Of all her talents, my favourite is her ability to step back, observe her own House of Mary, and laugh.

Along with other senior monks and under our teacher's instruction, Mary had begun offering guidance to other students. I had no intention of going for guidance to anyone but the head honcho, Cheri; the one situation in which I insist on being in charge is when what's at stake is my own ego – which is to say, *it's* in charge.

In my experience, once Cheri gets wind of an Ego In Charge – often well before the ego's owner figures it out – you can expect anything from subtle non-cooperation to head-on collision. An example of what I call Cheri's non-cooperation occurred after I finished the interviews with the monks. I requested a guidance appointment with Cheri, via a note on the bulletin board. She was leaving, and I would be gone when she returned, but she did not offer to squeeze me into her schedule. I knew from experience that when I wasn't being 'in charge', she could accommodate me in ways that seemed almost magical; within a fixed, full schedule, she would somehow create time for us to meet.

Now, however, the door was closed: her note in reply said that I could have guidance with Mary. I did not respond. I was in charge; it would be the way I wanted it or not at all.

One of the main purposes of being at the monastery was to get guidance. I'd come all the way across the country to be there, and guidance was slipping through my fingers. I lay on my bunk and suffered.

After a while, something shifted, and the problem began to unravel in my mind. I began to consider that I might be wrong in assuming that Mary was not advanced enough to offer me guidance. And under that was a different assumption – the opposite, in fact: that a person who gives guidance to another must have superior knowledge. For Mary to be more advanced than I was felt like a serious threat. I didn't mind her being superior in things I had defined myself as not good at, things in which I had no interest or identity. But in the matter of spiritual practice, I wanted us to be what we had always been, peers. It was as if the House of Sara and the House of Mary could be constructed with different materials but had to be exactly the same size.

If I had reflected for even a moment on what I'd heard from Mary in the interview, I might have been reassured: she clearly was not caught up in the superior/inferior duality. Which is not to say that she wasn't being tortured by her role as Supermonk and all that implied; the difference was that she *saw* it, saw it for what it was, and, in that seeing, she was able to stand apart from it. Furthermore, her openness about her struggles helped me see my own conditioned patterns, how I cling to incompetence, avoid challenge, hide abilities I think others might envy and resent. For both of us, it boiled down to the simple human desire to be liked, and the human mistake of going about that in a way that causes suffering – because it is based on a false idea of who we are.

OK, I said to myself. I see how it is. Mary and I can interact without any roles at all. The fact that she lives now as a monk, that she's in a position of authority here, does not mean we can't be together the way we always have, even if it's in a new context.

I left Mary a note requesting a guidance appointment. She wrote back that guidance was not offered during *sesshin*. The eight-day siege of intensive meditation, from early morning to late at night, would begin the next day.

Eight days of silence in which to contemplate not receiving guidance from Cheri, and – even though I had *let that go*, which surely deserved a reward! – not receiving it from Mary, either. There it was again, in the assumption that letting go would be rewarded, and on my terms: ego jumping in with how it should be, how it *would* be if *I* were in charge.

During the *sesshin* I had this insight: the point of guidance is not to get something special from someone who knows more than I do, to up-grade the House of Sara with spiritual furnishings from those grand Houses of Cheri and Mary. It is simply, like all of meditation practice, to see what is actually so in each moment. Guidance is a chance to par-ticipate in the still, clear awareness of another, which reflects not only the confusion that clouds my understanding, but also understanding itself – whether it appears to be coming from the person offering guid-ance or from me. True, the steadiness of the teacher's awareness makes it an unusually clear mirror, and someone with a lot of experi-ence, a Supermonk, will also offer a high degree of steadiness. But I can't carry around a teacher or a monk. Ultimately, what I seek is my own wisdom. Like everybody else, I possess the capacity for wisdom if I let go whatever is in the way – namely, ideas about myself and others, those mansions of ego.

Who's in charge, then? Nobody. Nothing, anyway, that could be called a 'self'.

The following winter I was at the monastery again, editing material for the book and interviewing Cheri for a new one. In the dormitory cubicle where I slept and worked, a casement window looked onto a courtyard where Mary supervised a work crew building a pool and fountain. She had done it, the heroic job: the monastery buildings were completed and had passed final inspection. The plastic sheeting was gone from the meditation hall, the dormitory cubicles were equipped with the essentials, the courtyard was landscaped.

On the other hand, inside the dormitory, the heating wasn't working. The thermostat, which I checked obsessively, never budged from fifty degrees Fahrenheit. I sat at my tiny desk cocooned in thermal underwear, a turtleneck, two sweaters, a mummy sleeping bag zipped up to my chest, and a down jacket with the hood pulled up, looking, I imagined, like a human-sized caterpillar. Mary strode around outside in a T-shirt.

At night I would lie awake, wearing the bottom two layers I'd worn during the day plus the mummy bag and two blankets – but five layers of insulation was not enough for my body to warm up and relax into sleep. I had learned that at my own mountain cottage in winter, it takes seven layers of blankets for me to be warm enough, and at a winter *sesshin* I'd discovered that seven layers of warm clothing would do the job in an unheated meditation hall. Six was not enough, and five was miserably insufficient. One night, after repeatedly considering and rejecting the idea of getting out of bed to add on the sweaters and jacket I'd been stuffed into all day, I imagined writing a note to Mary. I would say that I had discovered a fundamental principle: The Seven Layers for Thermally Defective People. That was funny to me; it sounded like something she'd say. Tired of being cold, desperate for sleep, ashamed of my wimpiness, I smiled in spite of myself. 'I could lead a Seven Layers workshop,' my note would say, 'except that it's one of those concepts in which the title tells everything you need to know.' I could see her laughing. A slight but oh-so-welcome edge of relaxation slipped into my body, carrying me towards sleep.

Mary never seemed to notice my being a wimp, or didn't care – or maybe it was that she did not believe that judgement with which I labelled myself. Another principle arose in my mind: one benefit of spiritual friendship is that, in weak moments, I can conjure up the image of a friend and instantly partake of the strength I know in that person. Their fresh perspective, their acceptance, their confidence and their ease then become available to me.

During that stay at the monastery, the monks' weekly meetings were devoted to practising communication skills, part of their training in leading group discussion and offering guidance. The jargon involved – one person 'facilitates' another's 'process' – made me cringe. I was invited to join them, and such 'invitations' are accepted; everyone participates in group activities, period. That was my first exposure to reflective listening, and my resistance was in high gear. I participated, but I hated mouthing back the very same words I had heard. I expected to be in charge of my own verbal expression.

Towards the end of my time there, Mary and I had a chance for a brief conversation. She looked uncertain, all of the confidence and competence I'd observed through my window – or imagined I'd observed – drained away. She was still leading the fountain project, she told me, but she was no longer Work Director. Her persistent need to be the one in charge put Mary at odds with the whole purpose of the monastery, which, as Cheri likes to say, is not to build buildings but to dissolve egos.

What would be a demotion in the outside world – hard enough on anybody's self-esteem – was for Mary a devastating blow to her identity. Seeing my House of Mary shaken to its foundation, and at a loss for how to respond, I simply listened. At some points I even repeated back what Mary said.

Later that year, Mary wrote me that she had worked through her Supermonk issue, and she was looking for a way to acknowledge that as a milestone in her spiritual journey. Ours is a pared-down practice, largely free of ceremony. If we had a mantra, it might be along the lines of No Robes, No Roles, No Rites – nothing special that could set some people apart. No shaved heads, Cheri had said from the first, dismaying at least one monk who'd had his heart set on that signature Zen look. In the absence of such indicators of a student's progress, perhaps Cheri agreed to Mary's borrowing the tradition in which a student marks a new stage on the path by taking a spiritual name. In any case, that's what happened. Mary became Faith.

Around that time, Faith and another monk began to lead meditation retreats. At the first one I attended, I had guidance with Faith. Accepting guidance from anyone but Cheri was one of many things in Zen practice that I knew for certain I would never do, then did and loved doing. All the fuss, the suffering, was, as usual, about nothing – or, rather, about the same old thing: protecting a self that doesn't exist.

Once my resistance was breached, I used guidance with Faith to pour out any and all concerns that arose for me. On one topic in particular, Faith and I had a special rapport: our brothers. Having siblings at all can be seen as a recipe for resentment. Older and younger, male and female, different looks and talents and personalities each enjoy their own favour and can thus engender envy.

Faith has a brother who is an astronaut. For someone whose identity tends towards the heroic, having an astronaut for an older sibling sets an awfully high standard. Representing the opposite point of view, as an older sibling myself, I might mention how dismaying it is to see hard-won parental praise bestowed so readily on the shamelessly happy-go-lucky younger child, who then, in the case of my own brother (yes, this is about me) blithely belittles my achievements and interests in such worthy causes as art, intellectual life, spiritual prac-tice, health food, and sensible footwear. That's my story, anyway.

Dig down a level and there's a different story. Not being pretty, I fell back on being smart. It was not a conscious compensation; on the con-trary, in my teenage years, I saw being smart as a liability almost as grave as not being pretty in what mattered to me, attracting boys, and I became quite skilled at hiding it. Later, I identified with the people who read and discussed and wrote books, and anti-intellectual remarks from my brother or anybody I care about can still threaten that identity. Of course, being smart did not require me to be an obnoxiously know-it-all bossy older sister, but I didn't make that distinction as a child and, in my own eyes, being a know-it-all was hardly my worst failing. Once, in a generous mood, my brother praised me for my 'total integrity'. I was stunned: how could he not see that I am the very opposite – a person who sold her soul early in life to gain the approval of others?

Now, I don't know Faith's astronaut brother, but she says he's an ardent Christian, which raises an image in my mind of people who come across as having all the answers – not only certain religious types but, alas, many of us older siblings. What's it like for my brother to have me for an older sibling? I got an inkling of that from this account by Faith (recorded for another book I edited), in which her position and mine as siblings are reversed.

> After I had communicated openly with my brother about my sexuality, politics, philosophy, life choices, etc., I got a letter back that I interpreted as basically saying, 'I think you've made some really bad choices, and you're probably going to burn in hell, because that's what the Bible teaches, and we can't accept you. Love, Your Brother.' I was very upset, but I thought and thought about it, and I finally realized that he showed a considerable amount of effort and care just in taking the time to write me that letter, and in fact, no matter what he *said*, he shows by his actions that he does accept me and love me.

When I received a letter from my own brother listing my manifold sins and wickedness, as he had viewed them throughout our lives but got around to telling me only in our late middle age, I was unable to take it as charitably as Faith had. We older siblings can be immovably convinced of our own rightness. My brother later said that perhaps his words had come across more harshly than he had intended, and that he was open to suggestions on how to communicate better. But, in my wounded state, I had no communication tips to offer. Of course, there's always: don't trash people whose friendship you care to keep, don't put into writing words you may regret, or at least, having written a letter in anger, don't send it until you've waited a day or two and re-read it. Not to mention the time-honoured injunction to check for the beam in your own eye before pointing out the mote in another's. But the older-sibling voice in which I would deliver such advice was a large part of his complaint. I heard my sarcasm, my superior tone, and I felt trapped.

I wrote Faith about it, and she wrote back.

> Aren't brothers just the most maddening, disgusting, ridiculous, ignorant people in the world? Which is not to say WE aren't all those things, or that we are – but – well, do you know a single living human being who's not arrogant, selfish, fraudulent? To which I'd add from my own personal collection, resentful and jealous. You are so dear. PS Doncha love these tools?

The tools, sketched in pencil, leaned against a rack in casual disarray and consummate grace. Faith hadn't done the drawing, but she had chosen it; it reflected her taste and my own, thus representing an important connection between us. My image of Faith-as-artist put her on my side against my brother's disparagement, serving as a counterweight against her own occasional streak of anti-intellectualism.

The tools also suggested another meaning to me, something else we shared, of much deeper significance: the tools of self-examination, the tools of the Dharma, which we were soon to put to use in a way we never would have guessed.

Faith called to say that she'd been kicked out of the monastery. Not for any egregious breach of monastic guidelines, nothing in the way of scandal. Cheri was right, Faith said, in telling her to leave when their teacher-student relationship was no longer working. I was surprised, but not shocked.

I suggested that Faith come visit me, mentioning that I myself could use some guidance. Her loss of status as Supermonk was irrelevant to me; it was as the friend from whom I have nothing to hide, and who seemed to hide none of herself, that she was important to me. She would come, Faith said, but rather than her giving me guidance, we could practise reflective listening together, both of us.

The first evening she was at my house, Faith taught me a version of reflective listening based on Imago dialogue, which the monks had learned and which they found helpful in working with each other. Intended for two people who are close and in conflict, particularly when communication has stalled, it provides a simple structure for getting at the underlying truth. Each person is invited in turn to tell whatever they would like the other person to know. They speak in amounts that the other can retain, a few sentences at a time. The listener summarizes what was said, asks if it is correct, and modifies it if necessary, until the speaker agrees that the listener's summary reflects what was intended. Then the listener asks if there is more to be said. If so, they continue in that manner until there is no more. Then they switch roles.

We sat at either end of my sofa, facing each other, and I listened as Faith spoke about leaving the monastery. It took a long time. The next evening she listened to what I would want my brother to know in response to his letter. That took a long time, too. I was self-conscious at first, worried that I might be doing it wrong. Then, as truth began to flow, I wondered if I would ever come to the end of it. I remember nothing of what either of us said, only the profound relief when the end did come, and with it the sense of having been heard, in full.

I really got it then about reflective listening: not only is it a key piece in mindful dialogue of any sort, but, in the Zen context, there is another dimension. While on the receiving end it is gratifying to be heard and affirmed in our own words, to reflect another's words without interjecting our own perspective is to practise offering our full presence and complete, compassionate acceptance. The very freedom from our own views allows us to experience the suffering that is spoken by another as human suffering, not personal suffering.

Faith soon faced a dilemma: she was invited to lead retreats but she did not have our teacher's blessing to do so. She asked me to help her examine her reactions, to submit what she was going through to the clear light of Dharma practice. We set aside a time for a phone call when we wouldn't be interrupted.

I had agreed only to provide reflective listening, but when Faith called, she said she would prefer a less structured approach – trusting me more, I see now, than I trusted myself. The fact was that I had come to see reflective listening as safe and manageable, a refuge, even, and without that method as a guide, I feared I might have nothing to offer. But I didn't admit that, and somehow we got started without actually deciding how we would proceed.

At first, Faith sounded so demoralized that I thought she might be backing out on talking with me at all. I felt an intense need to know, are we doing this or not, and if so, according to what method? But just as I would in sitting meditation, I did my best to stay with what was happening, listening closely, asking an occasional question, observing my own responses. And there we were, exploring her 'issue', I – without knowing how or wanting to or believing I could – 'facilitating' her 'process'.

She spoke, I listened. Step by step, hand in hand, it seemed, we entered old, well-trodden, yet still scary territory: how driven we are by the need for others' approval, how in our different ways we sell our souls for that. How approval must take very specific forms to satisfy us – admiration in her case, adoration in mine – and how it never satisfies us, ultimately.

Faith said what she hated most was feeling like a fraud, and she managed to feel like a fraud on either side of her dilemma. If she led retreats without the approval of an authority figure, she would be a fraudulent Zen teacher. If she didn't lead retreats, she was a fraudulent Zen student, in that she would not be following what her heart longed to do, not honouring her true self. Ego had her trapped.

A disturbing vision filled my mind: Faith spread-eagled against a wall, pressed flat by her suffering, an unrelenting weight against her, no escape. Strong, heroic, indomitable Faith was still struggling but, I feared, losing heart. It felt as if we had fallen down a mineshaft and were trapped in an airless, black space of pure torment.

Then I heard myself ask how, when, where she had ever before experienced feeling fraudulent. I had no idea where the question came from; it sounded like the kind of thing a therapist might say, and I was concerned that Faith might take it to mean that I had retreated into a role, into a less than authentic response. But after a moment she replied, her voice soft. Her mother had dressed her in frilly dresses and wanted her to be cute, charming, girlie. She had recently unpacked a box that had been stored while she was in the monastery and come across a photograph of herself as a child, wearing a dotted pinafore, one ruffled sleeve slipped off her shoulder – the princess every little girl is supposed to be. Soon, however, she had outgrown the princess look, and all hopes of being a girlie girl were lost.

'I just was not who she wanted me to be,' Faith said.

At that moment, I saw myself as a little girl whose long awkward stage, at its worst around age nine, was memorialized in an embarrassing photograph. Wearing an ill-fitting plaid jumper, the collar of my blouse gaping around my scrawny neck, I had crooked teeth, crooked glasses too big on my narrow face, a forced smile, jumbled features framed by horrid bangs and braids – a photo so awful my father finagled to have it removed from my permanent school record.

Not who you want me to be.

In a far corner of my mind lurked the idea that repeating Faith's words exactly was a stratagem that she would see as a gimmick, shattering our focus, leaving me feeling guilty and ineffectual. But the sincerity of my desire to be helpful and the strength of our connection in that moment overrode my concern, and I spoke the words.

'Not who you want me to be.'

Then another sentence arose in my mind, and with it, again, the concern that it was trite, that I might sound like a would-be therapist, that I should just listen and not offer advice. But out came the words anyway.

'Tell her, "I'm not who you want me to be."' Tell that part of you who has internalized your mother's standards, as I tell my father in me, *I am not who you want me to be.*

'I am not who you want me to be,' Faith whispered.

For the first time, in my mind's eye, I looked at my nine-year-old self without cringing. I saw beyond the awkwardness recorded by the camera to the world of her inner being. She was a bookworm, whose reading life was vibrant and impassioned. The bookworm had been sacrificed to social acceptance. It had taken me most of a lifetime, but I could finally acknowledge and accept that aspect of myself. The bookworm may not be pretty, but she has her joys.

Suddenly the dark hole of suffering that Faith and I had fallen into dropped away, and within us opened the understanding that, no, we were not and never would be who other people wanted us to be. And striving to be different from the way we are only creates suffering. Who we are is not only inevitable, not only tolerable, but just fine. Perfect, in fact, for the simple reason that it's *what is.*

It may sound exaggerated, romanticized, to say that we found ourselves then in a glorious field of open air and vast sky and infinite ease – we were, in fact, still talking on the phone – but that was my experience. It was as if we were embraced in the all-encompassing silence in which our friendship had begun, expanding outward in every direction.

After she had settled into life outside the monastery, Faith visited me again, bringing as a gift a packet of newly-issued first-class postage stamps with a striking design. There was no way she could have known it, but the stamps touched a tender part of my history with my brother, Dan.

Once when he was heading to the post office, Dan had offered to get stamps for me and asked if I had any preferences – a joke, since I was known to have strong preferences about trivial aesthetic matters, which he considered as ridiculous as I did his concern with saving money. 'Not those hideous pink and purple ones,' I said.

'How am I supposed to know what you consider "hideous"?' he asked, reasonably enough.

'Look for swans' necks forming a heart,' I said. 'Not those.'

When Dan returned, he asked if I would pay extra for a stamp I liked. Yes, I said, thinking that maybe he was beginning to get it....

'How much?' he asked. 'A nickel?'

'Definitely,' I said.

'A dime?'

'Well – yes.'

'What about fifteen cents?'

'I'd have to see the stamp.'

'How much would I pay for my favourite stamp of all time – a dollar?'

'Maybe.'

There it was, the conflict between my aesthetic approach to life and his economic approach, our mutually exclusive obsessions.

From that moment, it seemed to me, we lightened up on that particular conflict, seeing the other and ourselves as just people in a family who know and are annoyed by each other's idiosyncrasies, yet may come to accept and be amused by them. Shortly after that, Dan discovered some marvellous stamps, beautifully painted insects, and sent me a sheet. Our letters to each other began to carry another level of communication via the stamps we chose to put on the envelopes.

Here's something I thought would delight you, a stamp would say, *something we both enjoy. We know each other*, the stamps said. *We are a lot alike.*

But that was before The Letter.

Looking at the packet of stamps Faith had brought, I murmured, 'My brother would love these.'

'Send them to him,' she said.

I shook my head. I had no intention of making a move in his direction. And yet – the very intensity of my reaction told me that it would be a good thing to do. But – no.

I was running my fingernail under the cellophane to open the packet when Faith said, 'Don't open them if you're going to send them to your brother.'

'I told you, I'm not sending them to him,' I said. But my heart clutched. I tried to press together the edges of the slit I'd made. Wishing I could undo … but so much had been done.

Faith and I went off to a meditation group. I had hardly sat down on my cushion when I knew I would send Dan the stamps. Maybe not right away, and I might still feel the same hurt and anger, and he might not receive them well. But I knew the stamps offered me a way to open the door, or at least not hold it so tightly shut. My meditation was light and easy, as it had not been for months.

The next day I sent the stamps, with a yellow sticky note saying simply 'Yo, Bro!'

I was convinced that Faith's role was essential in my making that seemingly small but significant shift. Because the stamps came from her rather than someone else, I saw them in the context of our Dharma practice, of paying attention to suffering, with the aim of ending suffering. Faith insisted that such ideas were my projections and had nothing to do with her. I just know that she was there at the crucial moment, and when she said, 'Send them to him', she spoke for my own heart.

During those first months after she left the monastery, Faith attended retreats with Cheri and even a retreat led by the monk who replaced her as Work Director. Now, *that's* heroism.

While Faith was trying to figure out how to live as a Zen monk without a monastery, she and an old friend, Laurel, fell in love. Faith relinquished her monk identity, she and Laurel moved in together, and after some time they decided to celebrate their commitment with vows.

I was keenly interested in what Faith would wear for the ceremony and, having rarely seen her in anything other than work clothes, offered my services as fashion adviser. That's an example of sheer play between us; Laurel could have been (and was) Faith's immediate fashion adviser, but Faith and I enjoyed my trying out that role, just following the impulse, seeing where it led.

The real issue, Faith said, was refusing to succumb to the pressure to conform to socially defined roles. Laurel, petite and femme, sported a chic haircut and dressed for work in high heels and tiny skirts. Did that mean Faith was relegated to a butch role? The little girl who wasn't the girlie girl her mother wanted her to be had had the idea that since she grew too big and strong to match the feminine ideal, she must be masculine. But in fact she didn't *feel* masculine, and her partner did not see her as masculine. Adopting a masculine role was a lot like being in charge had been for her: a notion, not a necessity. And a notion that brings suffering.

I too felt the pressure of a feminine ideal I could not attain, and the little girl with crooked glasses and braids ended up with a protective veneer that might seem masculine in a different way. What a relief to talk openly with Faith about the measures each of us had adopted to shield ourselves from that particular pain of unacceptability. How would it be, we asked ourselves, to live completely free of that pressure, to assume no roles at all?

Soon Faith called to say that she and Laurel had been shopping for their dresses, and she'd found one she liked. Aqua silk taffeta with spaghetti straps.

'It was a stretch to think of wearing something like that,' she said, 'but I got over it. People already know I've got big shoulders, so what's the point of trying to hide them? I'm going all the way – I'll be showing some cleavage. A whole inch. Can you believe it?'

If I could follow Faith in her spaghetti straps, and Cheri in her earrings, and shed the roles that limit my life, and do what I really deepdown want to do, what would I be like? An out-and-out bookworm, certainly. More solitary, less social – but more open with people I'm close to. More serious and also more playful, the way Faith and I are together; and something that is neither of those, but in the middle – free not to be anything in particular, just to be.

What else? With a pang, I recognize that the only anti-intellectualism I have to fear is what lives within myself and I project onto others: that part of me who would reject the bookworm, the part who believes that to be intelligent is to be unattractive to men. I would like to be free of that.

What other aspects of my being have not been acknowledged, accepted, allowed?

An uncomfortable silence within.

I don't know what might be the equivalent for me of the taffeta dress baring broad shoulders and cleavage on a woman who thought she should be girlie and since she wasn't felt her only choice was the opposite. I can't get that much distance from my own identity. The challenge for me would be different, something I don't see clearly. Not yet. But an ache in my heart tells me something is there, something to be let go.

Faith's heroic work in letting go is an awesome model. It may be spiritually incorrect to say so, but Faith is freer than I am. I like that. That she has looked into her being so deeply, gone beyond so many limits – that's my inspiration, that sets my aspiration. I'm even coming around to some ease with that quotation on the bulletin board at the monastery:

> Those who [are] on the Way ... will seek out someone who will
> faithfully and inexorably help them to risk themselves, so that
> they may endure the suffering and pass courageously through
> it, thus making of it a 'raft that leads to the far shore'.

Now I see Faith as beautiful. The gap in her teeth, her big shoulders, her sturdy build, are just *her*. I would like to see myself as beautiful in the same way, accepting what is. I would like for my fabricated House of Faith to serve as a pattern for moving beyond, rather than remodelling, my House of Sara.

If I were going to have a spiritual name, I would like it to be Freedom.

Here, now: suffering, its cause, and its cessation

Kristen is too smart to waste on house and yard work, so we discuss how she can help in my office. We take our standard lunch, tomato sandwiches, out to the porch, and I give her an overview of my professional life. How in addition to editing, I drifted into publishing books based on talks by my Zen teacher, how I had naively believed that if you made good books people would buy them and money would come, how I have neither talent nor taste for business and now I am in over my head.

Kristen nods thoughtfully.

I explain that on top of my own ineptitude, my book distributor has gone bankrupt, and I am plunged into financial and legal complexities far beyond my comprehension. Before I can escape from that particular hell, I've been advised, I must organize all the numbers – reflecting sales, discounts, returns, charges, and so on – that I'd never paid much attention to.

At the mention of organizing numbers, my gut tenses, but Kristen looks downright eager.

'I think I can help,' she says.

I warn her that it's a terrible mess. And it's not just the book business – sooner or later, she'll find out that most months I can't balance my chequebook; I mix business and personal money, forget to enter cash withdrawals, put numbers in the wrong columns, add when I should subtract, think four times eight is twenty-four, confuse credit and debit (they sound alike, and debit sounds like debt, and sometimes credit is bad and sometimes good – how to know what's what?). For the umpteenth time, I wonder if I have some mental block, some yet to be named learning disability, like number dyslexia or Business Attention Deficit (BAD).

'I like numbers,' Kristen says, 'It won't be hard. The first step is to set up a bookkeeping system on the computer.'

I've got the software, I tell her, and I've entered tons of numbers, but I kept getting a negative balance. As I talk, I am aware of sliding into dolefulness. I feel compelled to confess that my financial turmoil has been going on for years, that at times I get things so messed up that I sit at my computer and sob in frustration and despair.

Kristen responds to my drama with equanimity. She asks for my chequebooks and bank statements and sets to work. She spends hours at the computer, going through files, entering data, setting up categories, correcting my mistakes. But the mistakes have long roots, and I am regularly dispatched to the attic to retrieve files from years past. Day by day, Kristen digs deeper.

I fully expect her to be stymied, sooner or later, by some incorrigible knot of wrongness. There's a glimmer of awareness that 'wrongness' may be my projection, fear of some unspecified but irredeemable wrongness in myself ... but it's easier to drift back to the familiar anxiety, worrying that Kristen will give up. Give up on me, of course, as I have given up repeatedly on myself in this particular endeavour. I feel doomed to perpetual confusion and wretchedness.

But Kristen declines to join me in my orgy of negativity, and one day the accounts are reconciled. Through the office window I hear the computer's ka-ching: *all the numbers balance.*

I want to jump around and scream, 'Yay! It's over, the nightmare is over!'

Then, right after the ka-ching, *the mindfulness bell.*

Silence for three breaths. I take my time standing up and walking into the house.

I go again to the meditation group. In the sharing period at the end, I long to describe what it's like to practise working meditation with Kristen, how I'm glimpsing the power of sangha one-on-one. But

I'm afraid of saying too much, of being too personal. Afraid I'll say something I hadn't realized myself – how much it means to me for this group to come together for meditation practice. Afraid I will cry. I say only a few words, aware of the discomfort involved in holding back.

5

I Walk the Line

Which Is Where, Exactly?

Insight meditation teacher Gregory Kramer wrote that even after years of intensive training, he still found his mindfulness somewhat forced in relationship with others. If Gregory found it hard, I figured, I could quit thinking it should be easy for me. Aside from the intentional dimension in my friendships with Susan and Faith, it seemed impossible to bring to my interactions with people anything close to the mindfulness I know in solitude.

Then a possibility appeared: insight dialogue, which Gregory, who co-developed it, describes as bridging solitary practice and 'relational' practice.[9] You don't need to be friends for insight dialogue to work; in fact, I suspect it works better with strangers.

Insight dialogue appealed to me in several ways. Bridging the practice gap, bringing the meditative mind more fully into social activity, sounded promising. Deep down I hoped it might shed some light on that koan I had been carrying around, that paradox: according to tradition, the Buddha said to Ānanda that spiritual friendship is the whole of the spiritual life, whereas my teacher discourages socializing.

Another factor was much more convoluted. In his book *On Dialogue*, David Bohm makes an important point about paradoxes. What we consider to be problems are often not problems but paradoxes; the distinction is important, because problems have solutions and paradoxes don't.[10] That idea overturns a basic assumption about life, that things are wrong and need to be fixed. But if what we think of as problems are in fact paradoxes, our challenge is to embrace the apparent contradictions – including the simultaneous truth of self and no-self. (I wonder if all koans don't ultimately reflect that fundamental paradox.)

The experience I recount here culminated in an acceptance of paradox – a resolution of my koan, if you will – that I understood consciously only much later. Interestingly enough, David Bohm's writing was an essential link in that process.

I knew that Bohm was a physicist who had been associated with Krishnamurti and that Bohm's non-scientific writing gained him a following in intellectual-spiritual circles. In the course of editing two books dealing with the philosophical implications of Bohm's physics, I had become close friends with the author, Norman Friedman, for whom Bohm's ideas had been transformative. Norm had shifted from a firmly materialist, rationalist, reductionist concept of the world to one that was deeply spiritual. Norm viewed Bohm as the source of his understanding of the essential wholeness of existence. In a somewhat similar way, I came to view Norm as a source of my emotional experience of interconnectedness. My connection to Norm and his connection to Bohm linked up at a particular point in my exploration of insight dialogue.

Gregory Kramer states that insight dialogue aims to extend to interpersonal communication the ease, clarity, and acceptance we cultivate in sitting meditation, to expand our meditation practice 'out' into the 'world'. As soon as I read that, I wanted to practise insight dialogue. No retreats were scheduled near where I live, and the only option was to practise the dialogue online. It seemed like an odd idea, but I was willing to give it a try.

In the online version of insight dialogue, participants log into a computer chat room and communicate via live online messages. That is, one person types something about what he or she is experiencing in that moment, and those words are seen on each participant's computer screen. Whoever is moved to respond does so with another typed message, initiating a chain of dialogue.

In insight dialogue, ideally, mindfulness stays balanced in a broad middle ground encompassing self and other, avoiding the extremes of a total inward focus, which results in silence, and the total outward focus of habitual social reaction. For example, insight dialogue is unlikely to include stock expressions of sociability to which neither party really listens. 'Hey, how are you?' 'Great, you?' 'Hanging in there.' 'Know what you mean.' A typical insight dialogue exchange might sound dull and affectless, even pointless, by comparison. 'I'm aware of some discomfort about what I just said.' Pause. 'What kind of discomfort?' Pause. 'Anxiety. Tuning in to my body now – pressure around my ribs.' 'As you said that, I noticed some tension in my arms and neck. Wondering if anxiety is contagious.' The information exchanged is low on content – or rather, much of the content reflects process, the moment-by-moment flow of experience.

Refraining from usual habits of social reaction allows us to become more aware of 'parallel' or 'background' thinking, thoughts that are not normally expressed to others, or even consciously to ourselves. Background thoughts commonly reflect feelings we have been taught to suppress: fear, anger, jealousy, resentment, self-doubt, desire, longing, dislike, confusion. By acknowledging background thinking, we bring into awareness more of our mental activity. And in communicating those thoughts, we reveal more of who we truly are; we reveal what is usually hidden. In the words of someone I know through insight dialogue, the process offers 'a connection that is unfettered by social habit, convention, or judgement'.

This may sound more like therapy than meditation, but participating in such dialogue leaves no doubt that it can be a thoroughly meditative process. As the same friend put it, in insight dialogue, instead of the breath as a focus, there is the open and accepting awareness of oneself and others. In one moment, for example, I might be aware of the weight of my body on my seat and tightness in my lower back. Then my attention might shift to my breathing for a few seconds. Next I might notice anxiety, a tingle in my chest, with the thought that I ought to speak to fill a silence. I let that go, sigh in relief, and become aware of others also sitting in silence. I wonder what they're experiencing. Then I might ask, 'How is it for you to sit in silence like this?' If the question arose spontaneously, I might notice a sense of opening, release from a tight internal focus, a flush of warmth in my body as I sense the connection to others.

In insight dialogue, as in sitting meditation, it's not that we are free from our conditioned habits, but that we maintain whatever stillness we're capable of as an aid to observing those habits. Meditating alone, we mentally tumble off the cushion into our fears and fantasies, the realm of our conditioning. Meditating with others, we tumble off into our needs to please or impress or control or hide. That is also conditioning. Then we patiently return our attention to the present.

A behaviour I noted among the first Dharma teachers I encountered, in various traditions, was how they would begin a talk, or answer a question, only after a long pause. I initially took the pause to be an affectation, or perhaps a calculated delay to ensnare the full attention of the listeners. Later, when my view moved from scepticism to the opposite extreme, veneration, and the same teachers were recast in my mind as paragons of integrity, it seemed unlikely that they would resort to such a ploy. The pause, I figured, must indicate the time required to convert their transcendent wisdom into the woefully limited language we shared.

Now I have a different idea. Pausing affords us the opportunity to let go of whatever conditioning is running our lives at that moment and thus enter into the present. The pause is a key element in developing mindfulness. Just consider the consequences if we all paused before speaking and acting: we would soon see how much of what we do is automatic, unconscious reaction.

The first guideline in the insight dialogue process is this single word: *pause.*

As David Bohm observed, what we 'know' is often nothing other than our own mental patterns projected onto what we see. That discovery is one of the most interesting, disconcerting, and potentially transformative aspects of meditation practice. In the light of that understanding, I must acknowledge here that the chat room conversations and disembodied characters described here are not literal; rather, they reflect the sorts of exchanges that have had particular meaning for me, as I remember them, and they suggest what I gain from this practice. They are, in a word, 'virtual'. The people and the conversations represent my version of what is important – which is, after all, pretty much how it works in 'real' life.

In a chat room, there is no one to see or be seen by, no sound except my own intermittent tapping at the keyboard, no movement except the appearance of type on the screen. Tiny strokes, clustered into characters, words, phrases, and sentences, arranged according to largely unconscious cultural patterns, trace a faint record of a person's experience at that moment. In the absence of ordinary physical cues from the other participants, it is astonishingly easy to recognize my reactions to their words; with nothing else going on, thoughts and physical sensations are experienced with intense clarity. That is, the chat room format is surprisingly conducive to the observation of conditioned responses.

I began the dialogue practice feeling like the odd person out. Although people in the group didn't exchange much personal information, I gathered that most or perhaps all of them were students of insight meditation and had attended retreats with Gregory. As a Zen student, and having only read Gregory's book, I felt at a disadvantage. Also, I had a different Internet service from the others, which meant that getting connected with them online was trickier for me.

The most conspicuous difference between me and the others was in the way our messages were written. Ah, cybercommunication. My use of complete sentences, standard punctuation, and capital letters to begin sentences and proper names signalled to the others, I suspected, that I belong to a generation – the Gutenbergers? – predating the digital age. I cannot be other than I am, I thought defensively. But that's not it: in fact I try to be other than I am a lot of the time. It's that in email and online chat, I refuse to abandon proper English in order to appear more like people who don't even know what it is. My standards – read 'my identity' – will be maintained. Ego has spoken.

Further evidence of my advanced years was my status as a chat room virgin. The first dialogue session stalled as I struggled to navigate the choppy waters of the World Wide Web to the chat room.

'I can't find you,' I emailed the facilitator at 8:04.

'just log in,' he emailed in return.

'How do I do that?'

'click teh icon'

'Where?'

'bottom of srceen'

'There are lots of icons. Which one?'

'green msn log o'

'What does that mean?'

'are you signed onto msn'

'How can I tell? What is it?'

'just go onlinea nd sign in to msn'

'I am online. That's how we are communicating. But I don't know what "msn" means.'

'micorsft network let me see if i can find you anther way'

Long minutes were silently marked on the digital clock in the lower right of my computer screen. At 8:10 the facilitator issued further instructions I didn't understand. For more long minutes, the other participants and I sat in silence. I tried to reassure myself that at least I was dealing with meditators, who are accustomed to being patient in trying situations (most notably, sitting meditation), and who, if they'd been at it a while, would realize that whatever discomfort they experience arises from their own minds. Still, how embarrassing to be the one holding things up. How I wanted to make a good impression! As the clock in the corner of my screen registered yet another minute and another and another, I knew what awful thoughts the other members of the group must be having about me, how they wished the group could move on without me, how they probably had some way of communicating directly with each other that I didn't know about and were typing sarcastic messages....

Then I remembered: *All I know for sure is that these thoughts are coming from my own mind*. The pattern was familiar: fear of being left out. For all I knew, the others were happily checking email or playing computer games or ... even meditating, as instructed. All those fears, those things I think I know, are in fact projected from my conditioned mind onto the screen of the world – calling into question what exactly the 'real' world is.

When I said that insight dialogue is a way of extending meditation practice 'out' into the 'world', there was a reason for those quotation marks (other than my being a crusty Gutenberger). The line between you/me, here/there, internal/external can become blurred in Dharma practice, and that blurring is especially – and paradoxically – conspicuous in the online dialogue form.

Computers and the Internet, commonly derided as a source of mindless, impersonal distraction, are used in the insight dialogue process for the opposite purpose: to call us to this very moment, to promote mindfulness, to share personal experience in an amazingly immediate and even intimate way. Not that this is apparent from the transcript of a dialogue session. What is read in a glance takes considerable time to be typed out. Sitting still, yet keenly engaged, the moments can be long indeed – long in the most positive sense, filled with the energy of attentiveness to subtle levels of experience. The solitude offers freedom from the pressure to 'be somebody' on the physical plane. The intense focus on real-time expression brings a vitality to the momentary experience. Waiting while someone searches for words is often a welcome reminder that the process *is* meditation.

The guidelines from Gregory's book are aids not only to mindfulness but to opening ourselves to ever deeper, more compassionate understanding. To pause and relax before responding, to notice the reactive nature of the mind, to be aware of assumptions and judgements – those practices make online dialogue a powerful means of deepening our understanding of ourselves and our connections with others. We were experiencing that directly in the dialogue process. *It's really working!* I would say to myself.

To my dismay, however, people disappeared from the dialogue group each week. New people joined, then drifted away. I asked the facilitator about it. It's the same in any meditation group, he said. People come and go, and only a few make a firm commitment. Soon, I was the only one to show up every week, and sometimes there was only one other person.

I stuck it out, partly because I wanted the discipline of at least once a week spending a whole hour in meditation, even an interactive form. Before each dialogue session, I arranged my seating at the computer to approximate meditation posture, placing a footstool under the computer desk so I could slide forward in my chair and sit crosslegged with my knees resting on the stool.

However, in the dialogue sessions, I was gradually spending more of the time just sitting and less time interacting. The same thing seemed to be happening with others, and at times our stream of dialogue almost dried up. I began to wonder if that hour might be just as well spent meditating on the cushion. I began to think about dropping out.

As a way of maintaining my interest, I decided to make notes on my experience with online dialogue practice: what I was aware of, what I learned about myself, my grand insights. Coming across that page of notes recently, I laughed to see that it contained a single line in all caps: I AM EASILY BORED.

Then a new person appeared. His screen name was Ron4Reel. The previous participants, presumably chat room habitués, I figured to be at least a generation younger than I am. Because Ron4Reel had almost as much difficulty as I had in logging on, I thought he might be closer to my age. Also, he asked the kinds of questions I ask and expressed similar expectations: that we clarify anything that's unclear, have a beginning and ending to the dialogue, receive responses to questions, show up every week – all those things seemed obvious to the two of us, and not necessarily to the others.

Best of all, Ron4Reel wrote in sentences, complete with punctuation and capital initials. He even made puns and tossed in the odd phrase in French. He was not only at home with the written word, he revelled in it. In the ardour of his relationship with language, I recognized a kindred spirit. *He is like me.* How we long for that!

And that, of course, is where Dharma practice ultimately takes us in relation to all of existence: to the awareness that the other is fundamentally no different from ourselves.

In that first session with Ron4Reel, he and I expressed our wish to relate to each other directly, without depending on social convention. We acknowledged the difficulties to be faced as we approached that unknown territory. Then we dived in, and that was the last I thought about difficulties for quite a while.

A vipassana student, Ron was adept at noticing the flow of physical sensations, and I quickly got the hang of it. We started in with his chronic heaviness in the shoulders, my chronic neck tension, then went on to notice the subtler pressures and tingling and tensing and relaxing that go on in our bodies below the level of normal consciousness. Bringing that level of experience into awareness assured me that we really were practising a meditative process, the same moment-to-moment observations that I might make on the cushion but had never spoken about. For long stretches we would sit contently, just focusing on our breathing, reporting what was going on in our bodies, and describing thoughts and reactions to each other's words.

Meanwhile, we were getting to know each other, in the usual way but in a deeper way as well, and getting to know more about ourselves. I liked it that Ron seemed exquisitely sensitive to slight shifts in our connectedness. Any suggestion of distance arising between us seemed to threaten him, I thought – then realized, no, wait … *I* am threatened by it. We both said that we hunger for deep, true communication – but I needed him to say it first. Therein lies one of the greatest gifts of spiritual friendship: how we ease the way for someone else simply by stating what is so; how we recognize in others our own deep longing, or see reflected in them our own capacity for honesty or kindness or generosity or wisdom.

When I asked Ron about his screen name, there was a longer pause than usual. Then he wrote that the '4Reel' part was to remind himself of what he is searching for in his spiritual practice, his true nature. My unspoken thought was a judgement, about the loftiness of his words – background thinking that I was not willing to share at that point. Almost as if he were reading my mind, the tone if not the content, he said that he had wanted to come up with a cleverer screen name and was embarrassed at the corniness, the childish sound of '4Reel'.

The urge arose to reassure him, to protect him from embarrassment. But I sat still, consciously relaxing, turning my attention to my breath.

The most respectful thing we can do for other people, my teacher says, *is to trust that they are adequate to their life experience. Not to interfere, because whatever they're going through could turn out to be a step towards their awakening.*

Another line of type from Ron appeared on my screen, in which the note of apology and subtle self-denigration was gone. The screen name, he wrote, came from a game he played with his son.

In those words, I read – imagined? projected? – a tender affection for his child that was almost palpable, and within this man I suddenly sensed the sweet innocence of a boy.

'I am feeling such tenderness,' I typed, then remembered to note the physical sensation. 'A softness in my chest and spreading out into my arms.' As I think of that now, I see that what I felt was, quite simply, love.

Because Ron had another commitment at the regular time set for the group, he and I began finding an hour each week for our own insight dialogue session, without the facilitator. The times that worked best for me didn't work for him, but the dialogue was important enough to me that I made concessions to give it priority. 'ID' I wrote in my calendar each week when Ron emailed me his available time slots and we set our appointment.

In the first of those emails, Ron mentioned preserving some degree of anonymity, and his messages were signed only with his screen name. I recalled nothing in Gregory's book about anonymity, but Ron had been on a retreat with Gregory and I hadn't, so I was willing to follow whatever guidelines he suggested.

At the same time, because I defined Ron as my friend, I wanted to know more about him, and I wanted him to know more about me. He seemed hesitant; he didn't refuse to share personal information, but he said he preferred to let it emerge naturally. To me it seemed downright unnatural to make do with occasional shreds of information about his life. Since the practice was a form of meditation, however, I saw my task as sitting still with whatever happened, not wrenching things around to suit my ego.

There were times in each session when I laughed out loud, times when tears filled my eyes, times when I felt those sensations in the chest that we call 'heart opening'. It's impossible to separate out what part of the whole experience was due to the process of meditative dialogue and what part was due to the chemistry between the two of us. From my later experience with face-to-face insight dialogue retreats, I know that the process itself is highly conducive to opening hearts, quite beyond anything I could put into words. But it was also true that communication flowed between Ron and me with extraordinary ease, like a river coursing through its banks but easily diverted into woods and across fields, creating new channels, then curling back on itself. (Well, maybe that's more my style than his, but still....) To me it seemed as if we were so attuned that we could speak volumes using *punctuation alone*. OK, I exaggerate. But this man was clever – with words, signs, symbols, puns, allusions, and his wit fired my own. (Our abbreviation for insight dialogue, ID, was the impetus for a spate of Freudian humour.) The very pleasure of laughter was enhanced in the context of mindful attention. But then, what isn't?

For that hour each week, I was vitally engaged every moment, a greater mindfulness ratio by far than I ever manage on the cushion. It is astonishing how people separated in space can feel an almost palpable closeness when they speak openly from their hearts, or, as it's phrased in insight dialogue terms, when we 'speak the truth, listen deeply'. The connection I felt with Ron soon seemed as true and deep as with people I'd known for ages. Reading in Patanjali's yoga sutras, I was struck by these lines.

> Experience of the finer level of the senses establishes the settled mind.... So does being attuned to another mind that is itself unperturbed by desire.[11]

One way of describing the dialogue process is to say that Ron and I served for each other as 'minds unperturbed by desire'. At some points I would be the one who could maintain the grounding and focus in the present and not be drawn away; at other times he performed that function. Each of us was willing to draw the line, to bring our dialogue back to the present when it strayed.

I asked Ron why it was so easy to be open with a virtual stranger, so difficult with people we're close to. He responded with an economic principle, something about an inverse correlation between willingness to risk and the value placed on a commodity. That is, he and I really *didn't* know each other that well; there wasn't much to lose, no matter how it felt.

One week, at a moment when a sweet closeness had arisen between us, Ron said, 'I imagine a hug.' A pang of alarm shot through me. That reaction revealed an interesting assumption: cyberspace in effect created a boundary shielding me not only from the physical reality of another person but even *thoughts* about the physical reality – and I had counted on planting myself squarely behind that shield. I might enjoy crossing boundaries, but I wanted them intact when I needed them. I reported the sensation of alarm but only later looked into the nature of my fear.

During our dialogue sessions, Ron and I increasingly drifted into the delights of word play. One day Ron raised questions about our playfulness. Was it appropriate? Did it serve our larger purpose? Or did it distract us from the intended meditative nature of the dialogue?

I like to think of play as a state of blessedness towards which we all aspire. On the other hand, I could see how play fitted neatly into my conditioned pattern of avoiding deep connection. Play often involves a shifting out of context and thus away from the present. It feels good, but it can be an escape, a way around the challenge to stay with an experience when it isn't fun. I recalled situations in which I had unconsciously used play to avoid pain or fear.

To Ron, however, I said none of that. I told him that I wanted to play when I felt like playing and not to make rules about it. Surely, I asserted, play is a supreme expression of being in the moment, being fully present, abandoning self.

Yet at the edge of my awareness flitted the shadow of a doubt. For a moment, I saw how the unbounded energy released in play is like a drug to me, and my attitude towards that unboundedness is close to craving. To admit that, though, might jeopardize my ability to give myself over to play, so I changed the subject.

'There must be a fine line in there somewhere,' I wrote blithely, intending to lay the matter to rest.

But Ron, not ready to abandon his own playful mood, responded in the words of that spiritual master Johnny Cash. Across my screen appeared the words,

'I keep a close watch on this heart of mine....'

Quickly I typed the next line:

'I keep my eyes wide open all the time ...(!)'

Ron replied with another exclamation mark. We were seeing the same thing: the familiar lyrics looked like pure Dharma.

Neither of us could remember the next line, but after a pause, we both began typing simultaneously. Ron got a piece of the last line out, and then I finished it up:

'Because you're mine, I walk the line.'

I had hardly finished typing when our more elevated interpretation of the lyrics was obliterated by an intense emotional reaction. Those last words touched in me a yearning to be wanted. Being wanted can seem like my deepest desire, and to have it uncovered, even inadvertently, made me feel vulnerable.

To acknowledge desire for, and fear of, emotional connection, and to share that vulnerability with someone – share not in the sense of telling, but of having the same experience – can draw two people closer to each other. That often happened in dialogues with Ron. Ah, but to share each other's wit, because it reflects a common frame of reference, is to directly participate in connection. In the Johnny Cash exchange and other such moments that arose between Ron and me, I felt our minds were one, soaring in mutual delight. It was delicious. From delight to raw vulnerability – the gamut, all via little letters on a screen.

Because you're mine, I walk the line. Later, Ron and I talked about those words, how loaded they can be, what different meanings they convey. As he pointed out, the concept 'mine' suggests attachment, and thus the illusion of a separate and incomplete self, which causes suffering. Yet some attachments can also provide the impetus for us to go beyond our self-imposed restrictions, ego in the service of dissolving ego, as my teacher says. For someone we love, we'll walk the line – which just might be a line leading to our own liberation. Another favourite saying of my teacher is that we will do for the love of others what we will never do for ourselves.

'Mine' can also be expanded to embrace everything. 'Because you're mine' might describe the shift in how we view not only other people but all of existence, the selflessness, the oneness we fleetingly experience through meditation practice: it really is all ours.

Experiencing 'mine' as everything, Ron observed, 'keeps me working at this, but also trips me up as it becomes in itself an object of longing, and, oops, we're back to the second noble truth': there is a cause of suffering. Within the very idea of 'mine' lies the pull of separateness. A delicate balancing act, to walk the line without falling off into illusion and clinging, and the suffering that results. Even in so harmless an activity as online meditative dialogue, between two people with the purest of intentions, spiritual liberation, there is that pull, those moments in which balance is lost to ego's gravitational force, that wild mind.

Ron and I had a dialogue session set for noon on the day before I was to leave for a week-long retreat. It put a squeeze on my schedule, but I postponed my last-minute errands until afternoon so I wouldn't risk being late for our online appointment.

High noon. A minute after. Two, three, four minutes after, and Ron4Reel had not appeared in my chat room window. Five minutes passed. I felt like a teenager waiting for a phone call, as if he were the most important thing in my life. No, not him – his feelings about me. Meaning, me. The universe had shrunk to the precise dimensions of my emotional reactions.

Ten minutes. Contemplating the empty chat window on my screen, I cycled through anger, hurt, worry. Then – just as if I were sitting on the meditation cushion, or engaged in insight dialogue – I let it go. And back it came: *Where is he? What might have happened to him?* A sinking feeling, and then before I knew what was happening, I was swept away into resentment. If Ron wasn't as committed as I was, I wasn't interested in continuing. Then I recognized the familiar 'I'm-outta-here' rush that so often arises when my feelings are hurt, especially when I think that I am more committed than others. Acting from that feeling had never solved the 'problem'; that was an old pattern I did not want to repeat.

I was still sitting in meditation posture, in the place where each week I intensively practised returning my attention to the present, and the habit was strong. I would just sit still and follow my breath, I decided. But that urge to walk out on an uncomfortable interpersonal situation had touched a current of painful history and thrown my thoughts, emotions, and physical sensations into turmoil. I needed a more stable focus, and I turned to Gregory Kramer's book, which I kept by my computer to refer to in dialogue sessions.

I began reading rather mechanically, but as my mental chaos subsided, my interest was caught by something I discovered in the preface: the original impetus for Gregory's insight dialogue had come from David Bohm. I had been meaning to find out about Bohm's non-scientific work, and since I was online already, I Googled 'Bohm' and 'dialog'. I quickly found a website with some of Bohm's writings (and just as quickly forgot all about Ron; never underestimate the power of distraction.) I read Bohm's words as if they were manna and I were stranded in a desert with no food or water.

> Dialogue is a way of observing, collectively, how hidden values and intentions can control our behavior, and how unnoticed cultural differences can clash without our realizing what is occurring....
>
> If we look carefully at what we generally take to be reality we begin to see that it includes a collection of concepts, memories and reflexes colored by our personal needs, fears, and desires, all of which are limited and distorted by the boundaries of language and the habits of our history, sex and culture. It is extremely difficult to disassemble this mixture or to ever be certain whether what we are perceiving – or what we may think about those perceptions – is at all accurate.

The further I read, the more astonished I was: Bohm apparently arrived at much of what the Buddha realized, though without the key tool of meditation.

> Thought generally conceals this problem from our immediate awareness and succeeds in generating a sense that the way each of us interprets the world is the only sensible way in which it can be interpreted. What is needed is a means by which we can slow down the process of thought in order to be able to observe it while it is actually occurring....
>
> Suspension of thoughts, impulses, judgements, etc., lies at the very heart of Dialogue.... It is not easily grasped because the activity is both unfamiliar and subtle. Suspension involves attention, listening and looking and is essential to exploration. Speaking is necessary, of course, for without it there would be little in the Dialogue to explore, but the actual process of exploration takes place during listening – not only to others but to oneself. Suspension involves exposing your reactions, impulses,

feelings and opinions in such a way that they can be seen and felt within your own psyche and also be reflected back by others in the group. It does not mean repressing or suppressing or, even, postponing them. It means, simply, giving them your serious attention so that their structures can be noticed while they are actually taking place.... This may permit you to begin to see the deeper meanings underlying your thought process and to sense the often incoherent structure of any action that you might otherwise carry out automatically.[12]

That a renowned scientist could reach such understanding directly, through his own experience, supports the Buddhist teaching that all human beings have the capacity for liberation from delusion. My mind leapt to the one person I knew who seemed to have attained some degree of liberation through purely intellectual means, without the benefit of any spiritual practice: my author friend Norm, whose book about Bohm I had edited. I thought of how often, over lunches at a neighbourhood café, we had enjoyed noting parallels between Bohm's physics and Buddhist philosophy. The scene played in my mind: Norm invariably ordering a bowl of black bean chilli and a veggie burger, both of which came with chips, while I ordered some exotic and chipless salad.

'Here, you can have my chips,' Norm would say, 'They give me more than I want, and they don't give you any. You take mine.' He would beam, and I would beam back at our little ritual and eat his chips. Our chips.

My mind settled into reflection on Norm, our working relationship and subsequent friendship. There were times in our collaboration on his books when anger arose between us, and each of us was convinced that the other was not only wrong but impossibly arrogant (I think I can speak for Norm on this point). Nevertheless, the central experience of our relationship – what I observed in Norm, learned from him, felt from and for him – was simple kindness. I admired how Norm translated the weighty philosophical ideas in his books into the personal realm, specifically in terms of how people relate to one another.

After Norm's books were published, he entered a reflective phase, and much of what he said, I heard in Buddhist terms. 'My purpose now is simply to be present in every moment,' he would say, and, 'If I feel upset about something, I look within myself to see what beliefs I'm holding that cause the problem.' And, 'There's nothing to be afraid of when you accept All That Is. I think All That Is is what people mean when they talk about "God".' Best of all I loved his saying, with a look of radiant happiness, 'I've been thinking over my life, and I believe the whole point is to learn to be kinder and more loving.' Many, many times, at moments like those, we looked at each other over his chilli and veggie burger and my salad and our chips, saying nothing at all as tears welled up in our eyes. Tears of understanding, I want to say, and the understanding was always the same: the importance of *human connection.*

Norm's conversation increasingly clustered around those simple ideas, and his repetition of the same statements began to perplex and disturb his family and friends. Eventually, it became clear that his mind was succumbing to Alzheimer's disease. Today his dementia is apparent, but, amazingly, if I mention David Bohm, he recalls enough of that arcane theory, including bibliographic references, that I can momentarily be fooled into thinking Norm is his old self. 'The fact that David Bohm lived made my life,' he told me not long ago. He talks about feeling Bohm's presence, a wordless communion, and his eagerness to be with Bohm in the afterlife so that he can ask him questions.

Whatever is happening to Norm's mind, there's a remarkable result: he seems to have entered a bliss realm. When I call him now and tell him who I am, he laughs heartily and says, 'Oh, I remember you. I always let you eat my chips.' Occasionally he says, 'Oh, you're the editor who helped me with my books. I could never have done it without you. You did a great job.'

I like the praise – but I love the chips. The chips represent our connection heart to heart. Norm wanted to give, and I was able to receive. The love between us is symbolized by the chips, a poignant reminder to me that deep connection really is possible. And that it is beyond words.

(Another koan: Where is the line between mental health and pathology? Between mental dysfunction and enlightenment?)

When I came across the reference to Bohm in Gregory's book, and then the Bohm piece on dialogue, it was as if Norm's loving influence in my life were manifesting once again. Norm himself is in many ways lost to this world. But everything that transpired between us years ago can be resurrected in an instant, through a symbol, a reminder, and once again my attention is turned to the importance of relationship, from which, to be honest, I have so often, in various ways, tried to escape. My friendship with Norm marks the point in my life when, in relation to others, I began to turn in a new direction.

Aeons later, it seemed, I exited the Bohm site and my thought-stream about Norm to check the chat room window. EMPTY. In fact, it was only 12:20 (in such a few minutes, my mind had ranged through so many times and places and people and feelings!) but I'd waited long enough. All acceptance, equanimity, loving-kindness had abruptly disappeared. I composed mental emails to Ron4Reel: *You know what I hate most about this? Telling myself not to care if you're dead, depressed, or disabled.* But it wasn't true. What I hated most was that his not showing up might mean *he* didn't care. About me.

I typed a brief message to Ron, forcing myself to expunge all traces of sarcasm, then I hit the Send button and went off to do my errands. As I stood in line in the post office, picked up my laundry, punched in my PIN at the cash machine, anger would flare in me, and then my heart would wrench in longing. Now and then I would see Norm's face, his smile full of love. It's all about kindness, he said, about being a more loving person. That's what's important. Rather like Norm feeling himself to be in communion with David Bohm, so was I feeling myself in the presence of and inspired by Norm. By the time I headed for home, I was fighting back tears.

92

I wrestled my laundry up the steps to my house, then dashed in to check my email. An apologetic message from Ron about traffic. Imagine that: it had nothing to do with *me*. Such blessed relief – from the desperate need for a response from someone else in order to feel all right about myself, to the clear space of just being, of universal all-rightness rather than personal striving to match a conditioned self-image.

Off and on for the next twenty-four hours, until I left for the retreat, I would be overcome by storms of tears. It wasn't grief; it was heart-opening. In my mind's eye I would see Norm's face, his smile, his eyes filling with tears, and I would be convulsed with sobs.

Long ago I discovered that crying just happens and doesn't necessarily require a story. Nevertheless, my mind leapt into generating a story, namely, that by not showing up, Ron (albeit unintentionally) allowed me time and space to experience at a new level of understanding the simple truths Norm had repeated to me over the years. Thus, Ron became, in my mind, an agent of my liberation – a role I wouldn't dream of imposing on my teacher, who, as far as I can tell, wouldn't dream of encouraging such a notion. But Ron … ah, the safety of the virtual … Ron is fair game, a blank screen, as it were, for my projections.

In the emptiness of silent retreat, the briefly, intermittently blank screen of my mind would fill with fantasies starring the virtual entity Ron4Reel. I would recognize what was happening and drop it, only to have it arise in different form, the mind rolling on, intractable, incorrigible. I would turn my attention to my breathing for hardly a single exhalation before an image of my dialogue partner would again take shape.

Ah, I noted with pleasure, *he resembles Joseph Goldstein*, whose face I had been admiring on the dust jacket of *One Dharma. So handsome and wise. It's the wise part, surely – of course – that ennobles my infatuation….*

But I had no idea what Ron looked like. Ron4Reel was a virtual entity, a product almost entirely of my imagining. Ron4Reel was my mirror, reflecting my conditioned patterns of interaction with others.

When the two of us were in dialogue, it was easy to identify a physical sensation, like tingling in my solar plexus, and recognize the thoughts and feelings associated with it, without any idea of acting on it. Yet alone in my fantasy world, the desire to act – to *tell* Ron what I was experiencing – was intense. Absurd! There was no way to communicate with Ron since I was on retreat, and why would I want to tell him all that anyway? But common sense hardly dented the urge. A sobering thought: how often had I acted from just such irrational desires? What would it be like to act from something else? What was that something else?

Then again desire arose; now I longed to tell Ron my insight about my irrational desires. The urge was strong, almost a compulsion. *Isn't the way to connection to lay your cards on the table, to open fully, holding nothing back?* I thought.

'Unperturbed by desire' – ha! But watching the desire, its origin, its pattern, its consequences – the watching itself, with calm, close attention – can bring a steadiness. Even as the ongoing mental movie rolls right on.

Now I am on retreat, I would remind myself. My job is to return my attention to the breath.

The infatuation passed. It's hard to spend much time in meditation and not notice when your mind goes berserk.

During and after the retreat, the subject of boundaries arose repeatedly in my mind, first in regard to the dialogue with Ron and then, it seemed, in regard to every corner of my life, my history, my very being. I saw how, in the dialogue practice, my communication exceeded the set limits of our sessions when I offered extraneous personal information, or slipped back to what had been said in previous sessions, even (cringe) sent Ron email accounts of what was going on in my life. When I was in the grips of communication compulsion, it was impossible to restrain myself. Words and thoughts seemed all-important. I clung to them as if they were jewels, reaching and grasping and clutching across boundaries of the agreed-on structure of the dialogue. In those moments, the Right Speech injunction, to speak only what is true, kind, and necessary, was totally beyond me.

The version of the Three Pure Precepts recited in our sangha uses the word 'restraint' in expressing the idea of avoiding evil. Restraint is not a popular concept in western culture; I was drawn to Dharma practice because I expected it to free me from restraints. But I could see how in the situation with Ron, restraint would support my practice: holding back from crossing those boundaries was a way of bringing my attention back to the present. At the same time, I could see how any boundary could potentially be a prison, thus the necessity to follow the J. Cash mantra, *I keep my eyes wide open all the time.*

Walking the line means letting go the fear of disenchantment, the fear that if we don't work hard at getting people to like us, they won't (and if *they* don't work at it, we may not like them). The task is to leave behind past losses and disappointments and come back to this moment and to the challenge: how best to be with this person, now?

To honour a precept means finding a balance between indulgence and denial, cultivating discernment of the middle way that leads away from suffering. The precept encouraging restraint is there for my training. I may rail against it, but I see more and more clearly how it functions as a fence does for a garden: the protected space supports a fruition that cannot happen in the wild.

And so I walk the line.

Except there is no line. No stable, fixed line, anyway. The line implied by any of the precepts, any of the steps of the Eightfold Path – not only restraint but 'saving others', Right Speech, Right Effort – is as wiggly as life itself, slipping out from under my feet each time I get the idea that I know where it is.

And still … there is nothing to do but walk it, embracing that paradox through practice of moment-to-moment awareness, a dance in which everything changes and shifts with each passing instant, a koan flickering with the interchangeability of bounded/unbounded, inner/outer, crazy/wise, you/me.

I bow to my virtual partner for his willingness to engage with me in this dance.

I bow to Gregory Kramer for creating this process and offering it for our practice.

Finally, and forever, I bow to my teacher, who as soon as I entertain the illusion that I've found some firm bit of ground to stand on, yanks it out from under me.

Here, now: looking at you, seeing me

Kristen arrives looking tired. I ask if she has enough energy to work. She hesitates. Then, apologetically, she says no, not really.

I invite her to take a nap in my back bedroom, at the opposite end of my little house from where I will be. If I were working for somebody in their house and needed to rest, I would find it hard to relax enough to sleep, so I offer Kristen as much privacy as I can.

As I walk out to the porch, I sense that something unprecedented is happening. I lie on the swing to figure it out. If I were working for somebody and needed to rest,... *I had thought. But that would never happen. Being too tired to work – or rather letting anyone know that – is not acceptable to me. If I were working for someone and felt tired, I would view it not as needing rest but as being weak.*

Yet the fact of my even having that thought, If I were working for somebody and needed to rest,... *seemed significant. Might it not imply a tentative move towards accepting a part of myself that had been denied?*

I see myself at Kristen's age: too depressed to function a lot of the time, burdened with being apparently grown up but not knowing what I truly wanted and needed. Not knowing to get enough sleep, not knowing to pause during the day, not knowing it is all right to be tired and all right to give in to it. Not knowing that there is such a thing as compassion for myself.

In half an hour Kristen appears, restored and ready to work. I tell her that her taking a nap is a gift to me, allowing me to see my resistance to the normal human condition of needing rest. We agree that part of our working arrangement will be that if either of us feels tired or sleepy or just low, we should stop and take care of ourselves.

Could I really do that? Especially with someone who is working for me? Maybe. Yes, maybe I could.

And maybe this is the kind of opening and softening we offer each other in community. But I quickly drop that thought. Community, even that of a weekly meditation group, is associated in my mind with loss of autonomy, giving up my preferences for those of others. The very word 'community' stirs resistance in me, an inner hardening, protection against others' power.

Before we resume work, I ask Kristen how things are going in the rest of her life. Teaching Chinese to beginners is not that hard, she says, if she can remember to focus on what she has to offer and not expect herself to know more than she does. Then she tells me about playing the violin, how she practises mindfulness when she is playing music, and what a different experience it is from her previous way of playing. All stress is gone, she says, and her being is fully given over to the music.

Then she reaches into her backpack and brings out a page of what looks like a poem, printed on a sheet with a faint background pattern of a musical score. I had asked her to let me see some of her writing, and she hands me the page.

> *For much of her life she thought she was just one note,*
> *Just one F natural.*
> *She longed to be a C singing at the top of the chord,*
> *or better yet, an E in an entirely different chord.*

Three paragraphs follow, a fresh, clever, moving account of a classic spiritual journey, concluding,

> *Her whole life she thought she was just one note,*
> *but in a moment of silence,*
> *she realized she was music.*[13]

I am not a musician, and I may never know that experience of being music. What I do know, reading Kristen's words, is that she is so young and so old. She is me.

6

In the Forest, in the Rain

Mindfulness slips silently, invisibly, into the corners and crevices of my days, blending into ordinary life without my noticing. It often takes a teacher, or a spiritual friend, to point out places where the sense of separation has softened, when moments *are* experienced in mindfulness, when my being opens to the joy of simply *being*. And it took a spiritual friendship to spark a simple but extraordinary idea: two of us intentionally blending practice with daily life by holding our own retreats, at home. Neither of us remembers exactly how the idea arose, but I think the seed was planted years ago.

Sandra and I had met at a Zen retreat. I noticed her right away; whereas most retreatants showed up in outdoor or even athletic wear, Sandra's look – clothes in deep luminous colours and rich textures, with handsome jewellery and strappy sandals – marked her (in my mind, anyway) as a more arty type, *my* type. There was something regal in her bearing, and when she spoke in group discussions, her probing intelligence and her skill with language were a joy to me. At the end of the retreat, we rode home together, beginning a long if intermittent friendship, conducted largely during rides to and from Zen retreats.

On our occasional visits, as on those rides, when Sandra and I got together, it was to talk. Mostly we talked about books and art and spiritual life. Our talks ran wide and deep, branching unpredictably in a myriad directions. At times it felt as if I were standing at the edge of an ocean of allusions and connections and insights, like darkly gleaming gems, undulating, surging against each other, striking occasional bursts of diamond brilliance, stretching into dimensions I cannot name.

Theoretically, any conversation occurs in partnership, but I attribute that oceanic quality of mind to Sandra, seeing myself primarily as a spectator. I suspect it is something innate in her that has developed through her frequent engagement with other people's creative intelligence. She is a playwright, and she takes for granted that a script is subject to a multitude of forces, from feedback at preliminary read-throughs, to interpretations by directors and actors, and reactions from an audience. She relishes that process, finds that synergy stimulating and satisfying. To me, writing seems essentially solitary, and collaboration is inconceivable, scary to contemplate, in fact. I have marvelled at Sandra's taste for collaborative work, assuming that it simply was not for me.

Sandra and I had been among a group of Zen students who, when our teacher could not come to a *sesshin* at the last minute, held it anyway. We students took turns ringing bells and leading walking meditation, and guidelines were established so that no one would need to communicate with anyone else. Everyone was on time for every meditation period, from early morning until late at night, and everyone followed the guidelines. Four days of silence. No writing notes, no writing of any kind, no eye contact. The supportive strength of sangha in that situation could hardly be exaggerated. The others showing up, keeping the schedule, sitting still, and staying silent was a powerful incentive for me to do the same, to do my best.

Until that time, I had perceived the teacher as a restraining force against which I could rebel, secure in knowing that I couldn't stray far, since the teacher was there to shoo me back into line. But at the teacherless *sesshin*, each of us had to find our own discipline internally. That was the first time I looked to myself for what the teacher had always provided. 'Taking responsibility' had always sounded tiresome, something to be avoided, but what I discovered then was how much easier it is than being dependent (seemingly dependent, for this is an illusion) on someone else. Thinking the teacher was in charge of my behaviour involved an undercurrent of struggle, whereas once I saw that self-discipline was up to me, what had to be done was accomplished effortlessly. It felt great. So great, so grown up, that I initially suspected my teacher of engineering the whole experience just for my benefit. It seems to me that consciously accepting responsibility for my experience is a crucial shift. I have to make that choice again and again, but, over time, trust builds that everything I truly need is within me.

Throughout that *sesshin*, the silence was almost palpable, a presence in itself. Leaving the retreat together, Sandra and I did not speak for a long time. When we did, we agreed that we wanted more of that silence in our lives. Years passed before it occurred to us that we didn't have to wait for somebody else to impose silence and structure. As that seed of trust opened in us, we saw that we could offer that to ourselves, through our own retreats.

Our retreats reflect our wish to live in a more conscious balance of flow and order. Unlike other retreats, ours do not mean leaving behind the comfort and convenience of home, and, most important, our work; the original impetus was wanting to be together in a way that allowed silent time for writing. As the idea took form in our minds, we saw that all our daily activities – not only working but preparing food, eating together, cleaning up, exercising, relaxing – would be opportunities for mindfulness. Of course, we've heard that for years – when we were away on retreat. Now, instead of leaving our normal routines to seek spiritual experience, we bring the two together.

A key element in our retreats is meditative dialogue. Sandra teaches a writing awareness practice and studies the A.H. Almaas inquiry method, which shares key features with Gregory Kramer's insight dialogue. On retreat, we let go our usual way of talking in favour of something we deem more precious, silence and mindful communication. Those retreats, I realize now, are a form of collaboration – in our spiritual practice.

Our retreats typically last two or three days, spent mostly in silence. Our schedule includes several hours of work in the morning and again in the afternoon, and because we both write, we use those work periods for writing. Along with sitting meditation, we practise meditative dialogue. We don't plan our retreats very far in advance; they just seem to come around, like the seasons.

We meet at Sandra's weekend house in the mountains, not far from where I live. The house is in a forest, surrounded by hemlocks and rhododendrons, facing a rocky stream and a waterfall. At this moment in late April, dogwood has sprouted its first tiny leaves, paired upward-pointing hearts in the freshest newborn chartreuse. They remind me of the heart-shaped leaves of the bo tree, which sheltered the Buddha as he sat it out all the way to enlightenment. Today, venerable bo trees shelter countless shrines in Asia. Sandra and I do not worship, we have no shrines, yet the air of this forest carries a delicate suggestion of a holy place, like the faintest trace of incense. No, not a place, but a holy time – the time we have dedicated to this purpose.

As in the Zen retreats we attended together, our schedule is drawn up anew each time. This is significant: the schedule is not imposed mechanically but arises in fresh response to our needs and the situation. Unlike Zen retreats, there is no wake-up call. We rise and have breakfast separately, and in silence, and then our schedule begins. In general it follows the following pattern.

9.00 – We sit facing each other on our cushions and meditate for
     half an hour.
9.30 – We raise our eyes and begin our practice of meditative
     dialogue, which may involve long periods of silence.
10.00 – We return to silence and write.
12.30 – One of us prepares lunch while the other continues to work,
     and we remain silent during that time.

1.00 – Lunch. We talk quietly while we eat and then take a walk.

2.00 – We return to silence and writing.

5.00 – Still silent, we have free time for yoga, reading, sitting outside.

6.00 – The silence ends, and we prepare supper, eat, and clean up.

8.00 – Sitting meditation for half an hour, followed by open-ended dialogue that often continues until we go to bed, in silence.

Whatever variation of this schedule we adopt, we do not always adhere to it completely. We no longer see the schedule as a restraining force, *in loco parentis*, as it were, just as we no longer see the teacher that way. Sitting meditation, dialogue, and writing are what we *want* to spend our time on, and pursuing those activities within the structure provided by the schedule makes them all the more focused, meaningful, true. The schedule serves our most cherished purposes. Why wouldn't we want to follow it? Well, conditioned minds have their reasons. We might want to talk or have a snack or take a nap, and we might do those things. But the presence of the other person is a reminder of our purpose in being together in that particular way, a way different from ordinary life in which we unconsciously succumb to – indeed, are almost entirely driven by – the siren songs of ego.

Nor is our environment as controlled as it would be at a retreat centre. Sandra's elderly cocker spaniel spends most of the time asleep, until we begin to meditate. Then he wakes up, walks back and forth between us, clicks his toenails on the floor, paws obsessively at an old towel he plays with, snuffles, and – most distracting of all – stands close in front of me, looking up into my lowered eyes.

A childhood memory arises: looking into the eyes of my kitten, this creature I love so utterly, and wondering, *Who are you? What are you?* It is the question we ask ourselves, in one way or another. The question with no answer. The question at the heart of spiritual practice.

When I sink into doubt and despair, my teacher advises me to ask the classic questions, *Who experiences doubt? Who is in despair?* She recently suggested something different – that in low moments I say to myself, *I am a person on the path to awakening.*

I look into the mirror and face the being I know so intimately, yet do not know.

❖

Beneath the placid surface of silence and schedule, any retreat has the potential for serious internal upheaval. In my retreats with Sandra, there have been two such incidents.

On one retreat we inserted 45-minute periods of 'real' work, clearing branches and debris left from a fallen tree, pruning overgrown bushes, and weeding. Our aim was to treat work as meditation: to focus on the immediate activity rather than the result, maintaining mindfulness of body, thoughts, and feelings. We would work in silence, stopping periodically to stand together and take several breaths, bring our minds to the present, relax our bodies, and recommit to our tasks at a gentle pace.

It was early summer, and we scheduled the first period of outdoor work from 8.30 until 9.15. Then we would change clothes, sit down on our cushions, and spend fifteen minutes reflecting, in meditative dialogue form, on our experience during the work period. The schedule resumed with our usual periods of sitting meditation and writing during the middle of the day. In the afternoon we planned to stop writing an hour early for another 45-minute period of outdoor work, plus reflection.

Sandra's relationship to work is somewhat problematic; in particular, she has a frank aversion to manual labour. But we share the commitment to face what is hard, and working meditation offered areas of aversion for both of us. In my case, what's problematic is being in charge. Thus the significance of my serving as Work Director (a role we borrowed from our Zen retreats) was less my familiarity with gardening than my aversion to being in charge. Telling someone else what to do 'brings up my conditioning', as we say, meaning that ego is uncomfortable, and the mind fills with reasons to avoid the disagreeable task.

That first morning we walked the few yards from the front door to the driveway armed with garden tools and work gloves and Zen guidelines for working meditation, our mission involving, ostensibly, overgrown shrubbery. As I look back on that scene, I am touched by our earnestness: spiritual warriors, venturing forth to confront our demons. Inviting our demons to meet us at that time and place, for the purpose of getting to know them – that is, getting to know us.

The morning work period went well. The season, the day, the warm air seemed to bless our efforts: close by, bumblebees pursued their own tasks, and in the woods around us, an ancient species of magnolia blossomed with ragged pale-yellow stars.

But at the beginning of the afternoon period, Sandra did not appear. What to do? In our tradition, part of the Work Director's role is to see that each person has what is needed for the job, including encouragement to resist ego's promptings – whether those promptings be to push ahead to the result, or do the job differently from the original assignment, or quit when it gets hard. But I had no idea what was going on with Sandra. What to do?

I went off to my immediate task, moving tree limbs from a big pile at the edge of the driveway. What if Sandra were asleep? What was my responsibility? I felt resentment arise, felt how it tensed my body. I would pull a branch from the pile and drag it up a little clay slope and into the woods, my mind briefly on the task, then riddled with worry.

What if Sandra had given in to her aversion and decided that she wasn't going to work after all? Alarm surged in my solar plexus: our joint effort would be abandoned, I would be abandoned, even humiliated, if she derided my commitment, my seriousness. I heaved a branch into a clearing and stumbled back down the clay bank.

Then, for a moment, my self-concern lifted. What if *Sandra* were humiliated, ashamed at having given up (as I would be)? That was even more threatening; what would I do? The alarm sank into my abdomen, ominous, pressing. I lifted a big branch. The leafy end caught in other branches, and I tried to jerk it free, tension mounting in my head and neck.

A cue to pause. I laid the branch down, stood still, and let my attention follow my breath. Where is my conditioning in this? I asked myself. *I don't know what to do, and I feel as if I should know, because I am in the role of being in charge, which I hate.* What's beneath that resistance? *Fear. If I confront my friend, she might challenge – or worse, ignore – my authority. Resent me, not like me, leave me.* I felt like a whimpering toddler.

What if, instead of feeling myself to be in charge, I considered what I might offer? If Sandra were sunk in her own conditioned reaction – shame, for example – what would be the most helpful, compassionate, enlightened response? Ah – to help her see that suffering is unnecessary. It was not my job to enforce the schedule or defend my earnestness, but I could point out that suffering serves no purpose and can be let go.

I freed the tree limb from the brush pile and dragged it into the woods. My worry subsided somewhat, and I was able to keep my attention on the physical experience for longer stretches as I moved the rest of the brush.

Our work period ended, and no Sandra. What would happen? How would things unfold? No way to know.

I went to my room, changed clothes, and since Sandra wasn't there for our scheduled dialogue, went onto the deck and did yoga. The need to know what was going on with Sandra, the need to respond, to do something – all that energy lashing me to what had happened and what might happen – began to abate as I settled into experiencing sensations in my body. Now and then I would glimpse the possibility that no matter how demanding the situation seemed, no matter how dramatic my feelings about it, nothing at all was required of me.

I was lying in relaxation when Sandra came out to the deck. She asked if I would dialogue with her, even though it was an hour behind schedule. I agreed, and we moved to our cushions where we sat facing each other.

106

We sat in silence, our eyes open, our gaze lowered. Breathing. At ease. Gentle movement of air on skin. In the woods around us the pale magnolia stars were luminous in the late afternoon sun.

We sat that way for quite a while. Then I heard the soft intake of breath that precedes speech, and into that full and empty space, Sandra released words for which I was entirely unprepared.

'I just realized,...' She hesitated briefly, and I sensed the shift. 'I don't have to say a thing.'

In that instant, all the drama I had built up during the work period dissolved. I almost laughed. I'd come close to accepting that Sandra's action did not require a response from me. But it hadn't occurred to me that she was similarly freed from obligation. I didn't look at her then, but I smiled. *Yes. Sandra is there*, I thought. *She just stepped into freedom. She's where we all want to be. Or rather, we are here. Not a word need be said, by her or by me. In this moment, this place, nothing needs to be questioned or explained or defended.*

Here is the resolution of the koan I had been carrying around, the puzzle of how to deepen relationships while maintaining silence: communication is reined in from the claims of past and future, from the habit of reactivity, to the stillness of each moment, in which the right words will naturally arise.

The other unsettling incident also occurred in dialogue, as we sat on our cushions in a dark room with a candle lit between us. Looking into each other's eyes, we described our body sensations, thoughts, and feelings. Our pauses became longer and longer. My memory is that we settled into such deep stillness that the normal inner agitation subsided, and we rested easily in each other's gaze. Then Sandra spoke.

'I see through you.'

The shock felt seismic. What words could be more frightening to ego? My mind lurched into protective mode, anticipating attack. Never have I felt so vulnerable. Not only naked, but transparent, *seen through*. Yet my body remained still. It felt as if I had spent my whole life hiding flaws that now would be exposed – although, oddly, no particular flaws came to mind. The terror lay in being judged at all.

We are here together, my teacher once said to me in what I perceived as a tirade, *and you act as if you are alone*. Those words had served as a koan for me for much longer than the question about deepening relationships (and surely apply to all of us suffering under the illusion of separate selfhood). Now Sandra and I were together, and I could not run, hide, pretend, or act as if I were alone. Our agreement was to look together at whatever was there to be seen.

Aeons passed before I found words.

'What do you see?'

Within awareness, attention may fix on fear and turmoil, but awareness itself is stable. I let my attention rest in awareness, the ultimate refuge. Something in me would survive, I trusted, however devastating the reply. I sat still, in total terror and in deep calm.

'You know more than you admit.'

Now, it might seem like a reprieve to hear those words rather than, say, 'You know less than you think,' not to mention words naming my acts of cruelty or folly or deviousness. What I remember, though, was a vast sinking, as if the ground beneath me had vanished and gravity along with it; disorientation, almost dissolution. What was it that I knew and would not admit? The secret seemed as limitless as the universe, and completely closed to me.

'Know about what?' I asked.

'About the spiritual path.'

A sharp hopeless wish to disappear. It was an impulse I had felt each time my teacher refused to accept my complaints that I didn't know what I was doing in my practice. Now I could not hide behind the student role; Sandra and I had become our own teachers, our own windows onto ourselves and each other. We may hide our wisdom from ourselves, but not from our teachers, not from our spiritual friends.

Sandra and I have practised meditation more or less regularly – dutifully, even – for many years. The balance of our attention has gradually shifted away from sitting meditation towards maintaining mindfulness in ordinary activity. At times, each of us has considered giving up sitting practice, yet we never do.

We wonder if once people set foot on the spiritual path, they are on it for ever, regardless of how long it takes to get there.

Get where?

We've both been reading books by Advaita masters about enlightenment, the once-and-for-all, ever-after kind, not the momentary glimpses that leave us tangled in longing. Are we going for ever-after enlightenment, we ask each other? My teacher says that one result of Dharma practice is that we grow up, we become adults. Jiyu-Kennett called Buddhism 'an adult religion'. Vipassana teacher Matt Flickstein says it's easy to find people who have had enlightenment experiences, but rare to find people who are fully mature human beings. Sandra and I decide that our aim is adulthood. If enlightenment lies further along that same axis, so much the better.

During one dialogue session, when I lower my eyes the shape of Sandra's head glows in afterimage against her body, like an inner being deep inside her, the same size but without surface features. I sense a similar being within myself. We speak through our personalities, but does something in that speaking come from these deeper aspects? The words that emerge in this meditative communication are so simple, so direct, so clear, so compassionate – even as they take us into strange territory, where we encounter unexpected subtleties and unspeakable complexities, pain and fear, awe and ease and joy. That is the fruit of giving full attention to what we say. After the dialogue, I think, *This is how I want to be with people.*

During a walk we stop at the edge of a lake. Fish turn to face us in the clear shallow water. They seem to be looking at us, as Sandra's dog looks at us, oblivious to our personalities, asking the wordless question, *Who are you? What are you?*

That evening, rain drowns out the sound of the waterfall. We sit in meditation with the rain. When it is time for dialogue, there is a sense of, why speak at all?

We do speak a little, quietly, embraced in the sounds of the forest, and then our speaking dies down. The rain stops. We continue to sit, our schedule abandoned. We sit in the hum of fridge, the chant of frogs, the murmur of the waterfall. Fridge hum stops. Frog sounds fill the world. Are the frogs speaking to us? Or are we, in our listening, asking them the same question the fish and the dog ask in their looking at us?

Frog chant fades into a few solo voices, falls off into single notes, then silence. Still we sit. At some point it seems clear that the last frog has spoken. We rise without speaking, go out onto the porch, stand in the dark facing the waterfall, the only sound.

The next morning in meditation, my lowered gaze is filled with Sandra's motionless form: the horizontal base, knee to knee, and the upright torso with hands forming a circle, the cosmic mudra familiar from Buddha figures. A Buddha before me. Buddha-shaped, anyway. I am aware of myself as Buddha-shaped.

In the final writing period before the end of our retreat, I come to a stopping place, put away my notebook and pencil, and gaze out into the treetops. Soon, summer will screen the view of the waterfall with foliage. But not the sound. It will vary, from a burble to a soft roar of white noise, but the sound of falling water is heard year-round.

Now in late April, the forest itself is revealed in all its ongoingness. Trees toppled in a winter ice storm pierce the space with fractured trunks, and the ground is littered with limbs. A few dogwood blossoms still fleck the woods with brilliant white, but most are past their peak. Against the dark evergreen background, the pink-yellow fuzz and slick maroon of new oak and maple leaves suggest a tapestry, woven on trunks and branches splotched with moss and lichen, pale green in the damp. This forest lives much of its life veiled in rain and mist.

I think about forest monks in the Buddhist tradition, their rainy season retreats, their bo trees. We are a world away from that; renunciants we are not. And yet there is a thread of intent linking them and us. *Who are we?* We are on the path to awakening.

Here, now: rejoicing in our merit

The meditation group that Kristen formed has met a few times at her house, but now Kristen's parents, Steve and Betsy, are leaving for several weeks on vacation. Kristen herself will be leaving soon; she has found a spiritual community to move to. The group will need to find another place to meet.

One member of our group, Russell, offers his place, or rather his parents', where he is staying while his house is being built nearby.

Russell's mother is my close friend Barbara, who is also in the group. I can't imagine being in a meditation group with my parents, especially a group in which personal experience is shared so openly. But here are Russell and Barbara, Kristen and Steve and Betsy, all participating, with what seems to be remarkable sincerity, in the presence of their family members. Other meditation groups may match our spiritual mix – practising Jews and Christians, Buddhists of various lineages, an Ashtanga yogi, a couple in a Native American tradition – but how many can boast two sets of parents and children?

On the morning of the first day we are to meet at Russell and Barbara's, I am in my accustomed place on the porch, writing, and Kristen is inside working on the computer. Jacqui calls to say she won't be able to come today. With Kristen's parents and Maggie and Alan also away, that leaves me and Kristen.

I think what a long drive it is up the mountain to Russell and Barbara's. I want to continue with my work. I wonder if Russell and Barbara feel obliged to have us at their place, rather than truly wanting to. I've had the experience of offering my house for group meditation and having to be there even when only one person, or no one, showed up. That was years ago, but the resentment is still alive.

I call Barbara and suggest that we cancel the meeting. I suspect that she has something else she'd rather do, too. Or maybe that's my projection: one of the bonds of understanding between the two of us is our chronic sense of time being short and our need to give priority to work. But Barbara says she will consult Russell. I don't want to come unless there's a critical mass of people, I tell her. Three, I feel, is not critical mass. I don't count myself; in my ambivalence, I equal more than zero but less than one.

With Kristen leaving, how many of us will show up next week? I do not want to drive half an hour up the mountain to sit with one or two other people. I do not want to worry about this every Wednesday.

The next time Kristen rings the mindfulness bell, I pause for three breaths, then ask her to come join me on the porch. She sits in the swing, and I turn my rocking chair to face her. Laying out my reasonable reasons, I say I am not going to meditation that afternoon. In fact, I am going to drop out of the group.

Her dark eyes hold mine. Her words are simple, but her questions gently penetrate my resistance, leading me to its centre, into my hurt: I am afraid that the others in the group are not as serious and committed as I am, and that I will end up feeling the odd person out, looked upon as a zealot.

But that isn't all there is to it. I am aware that Kristen must be aware that I am probably caught in a projection, so I might as well see it for myself. I pause – and there it is: the fear that I am not as serious and committed as I expect myself to be. The zealot within holds such exacting standards.

I tell Kristen my insight. This is not about the others, this is about me; I see it now. We sit solemnly. The human habit of self-deception underlying self-assertion and self-righteousness is painfully clear to me.

The telephone rings. It's Russell. 'Mom says you don't want to come unless there's a critical mass of people. I understand. But I really want to keep this time each week for my practice, so I'll be sitting here this afternoon anyway. Even if no one comes. Next week, too.'

In sweet silence Kristen and I ride up the mountain to Barbara and Russell's. The four of us arrange our cushions on the deck and sit outside. Towards the end of our meditation, a few raindrops fall. We consider where we will meet the following week if it rains; space is tight inside the house.

Russell doesn't miss a beat: we can meditate in their tree house, he says, pointing down the hill from the deck. Braced against a cluster of five thick tree trunks, it is agreeably close to the ground, with easy access via a short sloping ladder.

Nothing is going to stop this group, I realize. Neither my requirements – that we not meet on Sunday, not be social, not have potlucks – nor family members nor vacations nor rain. Just one person can constitute critical mass, holding open the door for the rest of us.

7

When the Student is Ready
the Sangha Appears

Kristen came to my house for working meditation only a few times, but she firmly imprinted my awareness with a sense of sangha. The meditation group she left behind proved far more enduring than any of us might have expected. Almost a year has passed, more people have joined, and the group has met every week, even during holidays when there were only two people in town.

Part of Kristen's legacy is the form and the tone of our gathering. We sit on cushions and chairs facing into the circle for half an hour of meditation, then whoever is keeping time leads us in half an hour of walking meditation. The same person reads a short passage from a Dharma book or other text on spiritual life. We sit for another half hour, during which anyone who is moved to speak does so, bowing before and after, with the others bowing in acknowledgement. When someone is speaking, the rest practise deep listening. Whatever is said is accepted in silence; we do not talk back and forth to each other, and we treat whatever is said as confidential. The role of 'ring reader' – the person who rings the bell and brings a passage to read – rotates among us informally.

During the first summer, we alternated between what I think of as our two tree houses. Barbara and Russell's tree house comfortably accommodated six people and seven at a squeeze. We would proceed down a path from the house, Russell carrying an Indian rug, the rest of us with our cushions and often umbrellas, a file of willing seekers. One by one, we mindfully clambered up the sloping ladder into the tree house and took our places in a circle. With rain tapping on the tin roof, then letting up, then drumming hard, then fading into bursts of sunlight and birdsong and bee hum, we would sit in intimate connection with our mountain rainforest habitat.

At Kristen's parents', we meet on a spacious roofed deck surrounded by tall red oaks, white oaks, poplars, and ash trees. Hummingbirds swoop past our heads, and the family's big dog wanders among us, swatting us with her tail. The dog sometimes barks at distant noises, but we sit still and quiet, making our peace with sounds from occasional cars and chainsaws, and even gunshots from a neighbour's target practice. In the winter we meet inside, where a venerable cat joins our silent walking meditation through the house and, if there's a vacant cushion to nestle against, our sitting. When the mountain roads are icy, we meet at houses lower down. Wherever we gather, we adjust easily to space, pets, noise, weather.

Today we met at my house. Jacqui, who was away for the last two weeks, said how much she missed our sangha, then hesitated and revised her statement. I knew what she meant: it's not 'missing', exactly. The one time I wasn't at meditation, I didn't miss it, didn't even think about it. And yet when we are sitting together, the silent companionship is so precious, so fresh in its hereness and nowness, openness, ease, that I am keenly aware of the mindfulness I miss in my normal life.

Jacqui led the walking meditation. She took us out onto the porch and around the swing, where there's barely enough room to pass; we had to turn sideways. I consider my porch too small for walking meditation; I would never lead walking there, but she did it, and it was all right. Each time she rang the bell, our signal to stop for three breaths, I saw my house – its spaces, its familiar contents – with fresh eyes.

When do we ever simply stop and silently, deeply experience our own living space? There is something magical about it.

Inside my small, dim, crowded dining room, we circled the table. One chair wasn't pushed in all the way, and Jacqui stumbled against it. I felt a pang of responsibility as the bell tumbled onto the floor with a clunk. But then I recalled an incident from the previous week and smiled to myself: the silence had already begun when Barbara realized she was still wearing her running shoes and ripped loose the velcro fasteners, making a harsh noise. Afterwards, I had asked her if she felt self-conscious about it, as today I asked Jacqui about dropping the bell. My assumption was that they felt what I would feel, mortified, and my intention was to reassure them. But to my surprise, both of them were nonchalant. They are innocent of the formality of Zen practice, in which dropping the bell looms large among fears of whoever leads walking meditation, and making an inadvertent noise is dreaded by everyone, and wearing shoes into the zendo is unthinkable.

I am grateful for that particular aspect of Zen training, though. Without it, I would not have known the immense relief when the worst has happened and I'm liberated from the fear of it. On one occasion, the 'worst' came to pass for both Faith and me simultaneously, when she was leading walking meditation at a retreat and I was in line behind her. I'd sometimes thought, *the others can take bathroom breaks during the walking periods, but what's the leader to do?* When we neared the door of the meditation hall, I found out: Faith turned to me, bowed, handed me the bell and striker, and left. I was very, very surprised, but there was nothing to do but lead the rest of the walking, with the sense of having discovered an important secret: oh, so *that's* what you do – whatever you need to do. It's a lesson that depends on the presence of others, a lesson you necessarily learn in sangha. You cannot make a mistake: someone is at your back, not to judge you but to be there when you need them.

Jacqui and Barbara and everyone else in our group have become my teachers. They support my efforts and refine my aspirations and enlarge my understanding. They have their own views, which bump up against my views and, as the saying goes, smooth my rough edges, round my corners, soften me.

Today, in our little group, the reading was on love, the injunction to love others. I've heard it too often, and it seems backwards to me: can you make yourself love somebody? I can't. When you get beyond ego, I'm convinced, love happens naturally. My attention drifted.

The reading was followed by sharing, and even though, as usual, there was more silence than speaking, it brought me back from my thoughts. I want to hear what each person says, and if no one says anything, I want to be present for that sweet, respectful togetherness of shared silence.

One person said that he plans to seek help for a serious problem in his life. Our silence deepened, embraced him, supported his intention. A difficulty is that he will need to leave our group early each week. He doesn't want to do that; the meditation group is so important to him, and he felt torn.

Love arose among us: we'll shift our schedule to accommodate him, we agreed. Love was palpable, anchoring my attention to the moment, to these people, my sangha.

Russell will soon be moving into his new house. I proposed that the first time we meet there, we follow our meditation with – what else? – a housewarming potluck.

I recently read a book called *Satipaṭṭhāna*, a scholarly examination of the Buddha's fundamental discourse on meditation practice.[14] Most pages have footnotes, and some have more footnotes than text; the bibliography is twenty-one pages of small type, and there are arcane diagrams that I don't understand. Not an inviting read, but I encountered enough that was meaningful to keep going. Two-thirds of the way through, a chapter ends with a list of ways to overcome or inhibit each of the five 'hindrances', or obstacles to concentration.

Eager to see what was given for my abiding hindrance, 'restlessness and worry', I scanned the recommendations: knowledge of the discourses, ethical conduct, and visiting elders.... I was about to close the book in dismay when my eye fell on the fourth item: good friends and suitable conversation.

Well – what to make of that? I looked at the recommendations for the other hindrances. Knowledge of the discourses and ethical conduct are listed for several, along with certain sorts of meditation, 'guarding the senses', and 'repeated wise consideration'. But the final recommendation in each list is the same: *good friends and suitable conversation.*

I thought about that not long ago when I was in a restaurant with my teacher and we saw a woman who has been coming to Zen retreats in this area for a couple of years.

'She lives not far from you,' Cheri said, 'and you have a lot in common. You might like to get to know her.'

'But ... what about our guideline not to socialize?' I asked, half surprised, half teasing her.

'You could always meditate together,' Cheri replied, unfazed, 'And you might also enjoy being friends.'

Someone asked me how I have been affected by these spiritual friendship practices. I hadn't thought about it; they are so varied and spread out in time and place that I tend to see each experience as discrete, encapsulated almost. But the question lingered, and into my mind floated instances of shifts, small and large, in the general realm of how I relate to other people.

Foremost in my awareness is this: the importance of solitude and silence. To propose solitude in the context of spiritual friendship may seem contradictory. But it is clearer to me than ever that solitude is the ground against which companionship blooms most beautifully. Likewise, it is silence that gives rise to the truest, most loving speech.

Those qualities are analogous to the stillness of meditation in which we encounter the fullness of the world. Just as our relationship with ourselves is enriched by mindful attention and simplicity, so is friendship.

Another seeming contradiction – another one of those inescapable paradoxes – is the importance in true friendship of leaving other people to themselves. By that I mean letting go the notion that other people's happiness depends on us, or ours on them, and taking full responsibility for our own happiness and knowing that others can do the same. My teacher encourages us to trust that people are adequate to their experience, and no sooner had I accepted that on an experimental basis than I began to see how well it works. As time goes by, I am glimpsing something much deeper in that idea. I think of moments when we see beyond the veil of our personalities – that realm in which we need so much from each other, owe so much to others – to the level of simply being. There we may watch our personalities as they dance, separately and together, watch them not only with amusement and acceptance but wholehearted love and enjoyment, yet not be in thrall to them, not need to do anything at all about them.

In the matter of Right Speech, I am fortunate to know several people who serve as models for me. Those people seem to view speech as a force let loose into the world, and thus refrain from words that might be harmful, choosing instead those that are kind, gentle, and pleasing. As I become more sensitive to harshness in my speech, there are more occasions when I regret my words. It has been remarkably easy in such situations for me to apologize. I think that's because the apology more often arises now from a different impulse; it's not to get myself off the hook or appease the other person, as it was in the past, but to reinforce what I truly want to be. An outward expression of regret can seal my aspiration to speak more carefully.

Something else I notice is a growing desire to cultivate skills that make for good friendships. Clear communication is one that goes beyond the obvious benefits of minimizing confusion and conflict. I am hungry to learn about effective communication; I attend workshops to gain practice in a variety of contexts. Another skill is the ability to see more clearly into the consequences of my actions, to understand the complexities involved in a given situation. I am surprised to find myself genuinely curious about ethics, eager to read serious writing on the subject.

In small ways, I am beginning to accord to other friendships the respect I bring to those with whom I share my spiritual practice, my *kalyāṇa mitras*. I wonder about the people closest to me who do not share this path – do they notice any changes in me? I hardly dare to hope – but maybe I'll find the courage to ask.

I know it is easier for me to speak honestly now in situations where before I would have turned away, avoiding communication that appears to be hard (read: unpleasant for ego). The more I speak hard truths, the easier it is, and the freer I am. Truth turns out to be downright addictive.

On a Zen retreat with Cheri a few years ago, the guideline about not socializing within our sangha was the subject of lengthy discussion. It's not that there's anything inherently wrong with socializing, Cheri said. It depends, as with everything, on how it's done. In our tradition, we refrain from casual interaction with one another because it tends to reinforce socially conditioned patterns. Not that it's impossible to interact with others and still maintain the mind of meditation, but in most cases that doesn't happen, and it's easy to deceive ourselves about it. Setting that boundary of not socializing is a way to take care of our practice.

OK, I said to myself, I understand. I can take not socializing as a useful guideline. It helps me recognize my tendency to ignore boundaries, and it helps me see the consequences. I'm going to stick with it.

Shortly thereafter, Cheri celebrated a major birthday, and the monastery mounted a previously unimaginable affair: two days of festivities, attended by sangha members from all over the country and beyond. Most of us had never spoken to one another, never looked one another in the eye – and there we were, dressed up, introducing ourselves, smiling and nodding, eating party food, telling stories, laughing, singing, drinking fruit juice toasts to our teacher. It sure looked like a cocktail party, and there were moments when I felt uncomfortable. But for the most part, there was an entirely different feel, something I'd never experienced before. Instead of adults trying to impress one another, we were like children having the time of our lives, utterly innocent in our pure and simple enjoyment of the occasion.

The free, sweet, playfulness of that extraordinary gathering brings to mind a strange and wonderful piece of writing by Allan Gurganus. The text is an orientation address to those souls recently arrived in heaven. It ends with these words:

> The Celestial offers you perfect, funny,
> erotic company, eternally.
> This is Paradise.
> This, my dears, is all God ever promised us:
>
> HELLO AT LAST.
> YOU HAVE ONLY
> JUST BEGUN TO
> KNOW EACH OTHER.[15]

We need not wait for Heaven. Here, now, many of us are just beginning to know ourselves, ourselves in others, others in us.

May we be clear mirrors for each other, for seeing who we are, and who we are not. In our practice of being present to one another, may we find inspiration in the words *because you're mine*. Not that we're in charge of anyone but ourselves, or that we can change things for anyone else. But because, as my teacher likes to say, you will do for the love of others what you will not do for yourself. Until you realize that 'they' and 'you' are one.

Notes and References

1 e.g. *Cūḷagosinga Sutta, Majjhima Nikāya* iii.206–7.

2 Greg Goode, 'From the Age of the Guru to the Age of the Friend,' www.heartofnow.com/files/other.writings.html#friend (accessed June 2007).

3 Karlfried Graf von Durckheim, *The Way of Transformation*, Morning Light Press, 2006.

4 Sangharakshita, *A Guide to the Buddhist Path*, Windhorse Publications, 1990, p.106.

5 *Saṁyutta Nikāya*, v.2.

6 Dharmachari Subhuti, *Buddhism for Today*, chapter 9, 'Spiritual Friendship', Windhorse Publications, 1983, p.87.

7 Ibid., p.92.

8 Elizabeth Cady Stanton, *Solitude of Self*, Paris Press, 2001.

9 Gregory Kramer, *Insight Dialogue: The Interpersonal Path to Freedom*, Shambhala, 2007. Information about insight dialogue is also available at www.metta.org.

10 David Bohm, *On Dialogue*, ed. Lee Nichol, Routledge, 1996.

11 *The Yoga Sutras of Patanjali*, translated and introduced by Alistair Shearer, Bell Tower Books, 2002, p.96.

12 David Bohm, Donald Factor, and Peter Garrett, 'Dialogue: A Proposal,' http://world.std.com/~lo/bohm/0000.html (accessed June 2007).

13 Kristen Wall, unpublished poem 'We Are Music'.

14 Anālayo, *Satipaṭṭhāna: The Direct Path to Realization*, Windhorse Publications, 2003.

15 Allan Gurganus, 'Toward a More Precise Identification of the Newer Angels', epilogue to *Plays Well With Others*, Alfred Knopf, 1997, p.16.

Windhorse Publications is a Buddhist publishing house, staffed by practising Buddhists. We place great emphasis on producing books of high quality, accessible and relevant to those interested in Buddhism at whatever level. Drawing on the whole range of the Buddhist tradition, our books include translations of traditional texts, commentaries, books that make links with Western culture and ways of life, biographies of Buddhists, and works on meditation.

As a charitable institution we welcome donations to help us continue our work. We also welcome manuscripts on aspects of Buddhism or meditation. To join our email list, leave your address on our website. For orders and catalogues log on to www.windhorsepublications.com or contact:

Windhorse Publications	Perseus Distribution	Windhorse Books
11 Park Road	1094 Flex Drive	P O Box 574
Birmingham	Jackson TN 38301	Newtown NSW 2042
B13 8AB	USA	Australia
UK		

Windhorse Publications is an arm of the Friends of the Western Buddhist Order, which has more than sixty centres on four continents. Through these centres, members of the Western Buddhist Order offer regular programmes of events for the general public and for more experienced students. These include meditation classes, public talks, study on Buddhist themes and texts, and bodywork classes such as t'ai chi, yoga, and massage. The FWBO also runs several retreat centres and the Karuna Trust, a fundraising charity that supports social welfare projects in the slums and villages of India.

Many FWBO centres have residential spiritual communities and ethical businesses associated with them. Arts activities are encouraged too, as is the development of strong bonds of friendship between people who share the same ideals. In this way the FWBO is developing a unique approach to Buddhism, not simply as a set of techniques, but as a creatively directed way of life for people living in the modern world.

If you would like more information about the FWBO please visit the website at www.fwbo.org or write to

London Buddhist Centre	Aryaloka	Sydney Buddhist Centre
51 Roman Road	14 Heartwood Circle	24 Enmore Road
London	Newmarket NH 03857	Sydney NSW 2042
E2 0HU	USA	Australia
UK		